PRAISE FOR *WOLFE AT QUEBEC*

"Hibbert has produced one of the most readable action stories I know. . . . He keeps one aware of a great deal without bewildering; his book is as factual as it is entertaining." —*New Statesman*

"Hibbert's portrait of Wolfe is eminently fair, without being fulsome; and the narrative skill with which he depicts the combined military and naval operations is admirable. . . . Hibbert is a real acquisition to the field of popular, but sound, history." —*Times Literary Supplement*

"This engrossing account, based to a considerable extent upon new historical evidence, is enlivened by perceptive character studies of the principle participants, especially of General Wolfe. . . . This is popularly written history at its best. Hibbert has brilliantly demonstrated that painstaking research need not impair the spirit that infuses good historical writing. Wolfe at Quebec is unfailingly entertaining." —*The New York Herald Tribune Book Review*

"Fascinating in the highest degree. . . . Hibbert's scholarship, while vast, is nowhere obtrusive." —*Kirkus Reviews*

"[A] convincing picture of the introspective, egotistic, fantastically industrious, and pathologically ambitious Wolfe. . . . [The author] gives an undoubtedly realistic picture of warfare—without glamour, but with plenty of scurvy, dysentery, brutality, dishonesty (in high and low places), and deadly, continuous, unrelieved discomfort; of white men and Indians engaged in competitive scalping; of muddled commanders and vicious rivalries; of women stripped to the waist and whipped through the streets of Quebec for selling rum to drunken soldiery." —*The Saturday Review*

"Hibbert has ransacked old diaries, letters, log-books for any detail that will bring Wolfe's great and final year to life. The result is brilliantly exciting." —*Sunday Express* (London)

MILITARY HISTORY

Wolfe at Quebec
The Destruction of Lord Raglan: A Tragedy of the Crimean War
Corunna
The Battle of Arnhem
Agincourt
Redcoats and Rebels: The War for America, 1770–1781
Cavaliers and Roundheads: The English at War, 1642–1649

HISTORY

King Mob: Lord George Gordon and the Riots of 1780
The Roots of Evil: A Social History of Crime and Punishment
The Court at Windsor: A Domestic History
The Grand Tour
London: The Biography of a City
The Dragon Wakes: China and the West, 1793–1911
The Rise and Fall of the House of Medici
The Great Mutiny: India 1857
The French Revolution
Rome: The Biography of a City
The English: A Social History 1066–1945
Venice: The Biography of a City
Florence: The Biography of a City

BIOGRAPHIES

Benito Mussolini: The Rise and Fall of Il Duce
Garibaldi and His Enemies: The Clash of Arms
and Personalities in the Making of Italy
The Making of Charles Dickens
Charles I
The Personal History of Samuel Johnson
George IV: Prince of Wales, 1762–1811
George IV: Regent and King, 1811–1830
Edward VII: A Portrait
Queen Victoria in Her Letters and Journals
The Virgin Queen: The Personal History of Elizabeth I
Nelson: A Personal History
Wellington: A Personal History
George III: A Personal History

JAMES WOLFE

An engraving by Richard Houston after Hervey Smith

Wolfe at Quebec

The Man Who Won the French and Indian War

Christopher Hibbert

Cooper Square Press

First Cooper Square Press edition 1999

This Cooper Square Press paperback edition of *Wolfe at Quebec* is an unabridged republication of the edition first published in New York in 1959. It is reprinted by arrangement with the author.

Published by Cooper Square Press,
An Imprint of Rowman & Littlefield Publishers, Inc.
150 Fifth Avenue, Suite 911
New York, New York 10011

Distributed by National Book Network

Library of Congress Cataloging-in-Publication Data

Hibbert, Christopher, 1924–
    Wolfe at Quebec / by Christopher Hibbert. —1st Cooper Square Press ed.
      p.   cm.
    Originally published: Cleveland ; New York : World Pub. Co., 1959.
    Includes bibliographical references and index.
    ISBN 0-8154-1016-6 (pbk. : alk. paper)
    1. Quebec Campaign, 1759. 2. Wolfe, James, 1727–1759.   I. Title.
    E199.H54   1999
    973.2'6—dc21   99–32509
                                                                        CIP

⊖™ The paper used in this publication meets the minimum requirements of American National Standard for Information Sciences—Permanence of Paper for Printed Library Materials, ANSI/NISO Z39.48–1992.
Manufactured in the United States of America.

For James

MAPS

"I never served so disagreeable a campaign as this....It is war of the worst shape."

BRIGADIER-GENERAL
THE HON. GEORGE TOWNSHEND

NOTE

THE capture of Quebec in 1759 has been described as the most fateful, dramatic and important event in the history of the eighteenth century.

In describing the events of the siege and the battle on the Plains of Abraham which ended it, I have consulted various original sources which were not available when the previous accounts were written. The story which has emerged may therefore in some respects be an unfamiliar one. The incidental portrait of Wolfe is, I believe, certainly so.

For their help in finding the diaries, despatches, orders, documents, letters, journals and ships' logs on which the account of the operations is based, I am most grateful to the staffs of the British Museum, the Public Record Office, the National Register of Archives and the National Maritime Museum.

I am also most grateful to Mrs I. M. B. Dobell, Associate Historian at the McCord Museum of McGill University for information and photostats she has been kind enough to send me from Canada, and to M. Pierre Renaud for several extracts from French archives in Paris. Through the courtesy of Colonel G. H. G. Anderson, C.B.E., D.S.O., M.C. and the National Trust I have been able to make use of the library at Quebec House. Mr Aubrey Beese, the librarian of the Oxford and Cambridge University Club and Mr Stanley H. Horrocks and the staff of the Central Public Library, Reading have been most helpful in obtaining for me, from other libraries, books not available in their own.

For kindly allowing me to copy and quote from the collection of Wolfe's letters in the possession of his family

I am indebted to Major J. R. O'B. Warde. I should also like to thank Dr Charles Joiner, Dr A. J. Salmon and Dr G. F. Vaughan for their suggestions about Wolfe's illnesses and psychological disturbances; Mr R. W. Ketton-Cremer and the Rt Hon Marquess Townshend for their help concerning the caricatures of the Hon. George Townshend; Lieutenant-Colonel Rex Whitworth, M.B.E. for some assistance with the problem of Wolfe's early appointments, and Major Freddie Myatt, M.C. for information regarding the regiments involved in the siege. Miss Mary Cosh has corrected several errors of punctuation and phrasing in the original manuscript. And my wife has given me constant help and advice.

The book is intended, not so much as a work of scholarship, as one of entertainment for the general reader, and I have accordingly omitted all references to sources in the text. A list is, however, given of the principal sources in the bibliography.

CHRISTOPHER HIBBERT

I

'**M**AD, is he?' said the King. 'Then I hope he will bite some of my other generals.'

It was the fussy, nervous Duke of Newcastle, the nominal head of the Government which Pitt was so galvanically running, who had warned George II against the appointment of the eccentric brigadier to a command of such importance. Wolfe was, after all, the Duke complained, only thirty-two and had never commanded an army before. How could he explain away the necessity for promoting to major-general, over the heads of so many other brigadiers of far greater seniority and more distinguished birth, a man who was as strange as he was conceited? It would be a grave error to suppose that there would not be serious trouble and bitterness in the Army. Wolfe was a good training officer, an excellent battalion commander, and by all accounts very courageous, but he had neither the experience nor the qualifications to lead an army. Besides, it had been reported more than once that the man was not quite sane.

The verdict was understandable. Wolfe was decidedly odd. He had, in the first place, a curious face and figure for a soldier. He was extremely tall and excessively thin. His gait was gangling and his movements were awkward. Some years before he had given up wearing the military wig favoured by most gentlemen in his profession and now, except on formal occasions, wore his own bright red hair, loose and rather long. His nose was thin and pointed, his jaw undershot to the verge of deformity, his pale blue eyes were strangely prominent, his pallor alarming. Unnaturally long and tapering fingers picked constantly at his cuffs and the buttons of his coat. An unusual appearance and a frail physique were at least partly responsible for a difficult and unconventional temperament. He was touchy, imperious, moody, vain, and heroically brave.

He looked ill and indeed he was ill. He complained of chronic rheumatism and frequent attacks of scurvy, and the numerous drugs and potions he took, including a medicine composed almost entirely of soap, seemed to aggravate the malignant disease of the kidneys and bladder which they were intended to cure. He was frequently in pain, often depressed to the state of despair. But even in these moods of deep depression he knew that 'the world', as Horace Walpole put it, 'could not expect more from him than he thought himself capable of performing'. His opinion of his own talents was undoubtedly prodigious. 'If ever my opinion of myself', he once told his mother, 'differs from my father's, 'tis certain to be in my own favour. I don't believe he ever thought better of me than I do of myself.' He was considered to be, he informed her in another letter, 'one of the best officers of my rank in the service'. This, however, did not mean much, for there were so few officers in the Army of any merit at all; and 'the comparison would do a man of genius very little honour'. The officers of his acquaintance were, in fact, 'persons of so little application to business and have been so ill-educated, that it must not surprise you to hear that a man of common industry is in reputation amongst them'.

Low as his opinion of the officers was, it was matched by the deep contempt in which he held most of the men who served under them. They were 'rascals and *canaille*', he told the Duke of Richmond, a young subaltern in his regiment, 'terrible dogs to look at'. After a minor engagement in the '45 rebellion, he decided that he had 'but a very mean opinion of the infantry in courage. I know their discipline to be bad and their valour precarious. They are easily put into disorder and hard to recover out of it. They

2

frequently kill their officers through fear, and murder one another in their confusion. Their shameful behaviour . . . clearly denotes the extreme ignorance of the officers, and the disobedient and dastardly spirit of the men.' He believed that 'no nation ever paid so many bad soldiers at so high a rate'.

His own pre-eminence was achieved, he knew, by constant application to his duty. He was not only one of the best officers of his rank in the Army, he was certainly its most hard-working. While his fellow-officers drank and gambled, went hunting or whoring, he stayed in his quarters studying military history, manuals of tactics, mathematics, and Latin. He did not gamble, drank hardly at all, and disliked playing cards. He rarely dined out, seeming quite content to take the plain mess food as he found it, without either pleasure or complaint. Having little money to spend, he had even less inclination to spend it. 'I have the talent for heaping up wealth,' he assured his parents. 'And the temptation must be very great when I am persuaded to part with it.'

'Our acting commander here', Captain Macrae wrote of him when he was commanding his regiment in Scotland at the age of twenty-two, 'is a paragon. He neither drinks, curses, gambles nor runs after women.'

His only interests, apart from his work and the writing of long, introspective, and rather boring letters, were solitary sports. He enjoyed shooting and fishing, and when he could not be at war or be watching 'a collection of well-looking men, uniformly clad and performing their exercise with grace and order', than which he found 'nothing more entertaining', he was never so happy as he was when he walked alone across the moors with a gun under his arm and his adored dogs at his heels. 'The country diversions will give you health and strength,' he advised the Duke of Richmond. 'They are the becoming recreations of a soldier, inuring him to fatigue—gaming, eating and the pox are the vices of the effeminate and flagitious; and have loosened

3

the morals and ruined the constitution of half our country-men.'

With women he was rarely at his ease and never appeared unduly fond of their company. 'I am often surprised', he once wrote with a regretful innocence to his domineering, possessive mother, who strongly encouraged her son in the attitude, 'at the little sensibility I feel in myself at the sight of the fairest and finest females.'

He was sure he would never meet a woman who could put him in danger of believing that life without her would be unbearable. Infatuations of this sort were not for him. There must be nothing in his life that might prevent him from achieving fame and distinction in his profession, which was all that really mattered for him and all he really wanted. 'I had much rather listen to the drum and the trumpet', he admitted in a letter which left no room for doubt where his true interests lay, 'than any softer sound whatever.'

For as long as he could remember the life of a soldier had seemed the only life worth living.

He was born at Westerham in Kent on 2 January, 1727 into a military household. His father, a bluff and silent man of Anglo-Irish stock who had married the daughter of a Yorkshire squire, was a colonel in the Marines and he hoped that both his sons would become soldiers also. Neither of them considered any other career.

At the age of thirteen his younger son James, despite his mother's entreaties and his father's half-hearted protests, got himself attached to Colonel Wolfe's regiment as a volunteer. The regiment was just about to sail on the abortive expedition against the Spanish fortress of Cartagena, and James was determined to go with it. But he was taken ill when he arrived at camp on the Isle of Wight and had to be sent home where his mother doctored him, if her recipe book is to be relied upon, with a nauseating medicine composed of the juice and shells of garden snails, green earth worms, agrimony, bear's feet, hartshorn, barberry brake, saffron and red dock roots.

His disappointment at missing his first chance of service was extreme, but it was short-lived. Less than two years later, after an impatiently suffered education at Westerham and at a school for the sons of officers at Greenwich, where the family now lived, he received his longed-for commission in his father's regiment. A few months later he joined Durore's Regiment, the 12th Foot, as an ensign.

The fifteen-year-old officer was at once recognized as a boy of outstanding application. His determination to become proficient was almost pathetic in its single-minded intensity. By the time he was sixteen he was his battalion's adjutant and was fighting at Dettingen. Two years later he was brigade-major and during the Jacobite rebellion of '45 he was aide-de-camp to the brutish General 'Hangman' Hawley, whose frequently heartless orders were passed on with apparent approval by his delicate young assistant. On one well-remembered occasion Major Wolfe was sent by General Hawley to tell a Mrs Gordon, whose house the General had decided to occupy as his headquarters, that all her property with the exception of her clothes must be forfeited to the English army. Mrs Gordon was a Jacobite sympathizer, and the young major did not trouble to behave politely. According to Mrs Gordon's account at least, he carried out his orders with arrogance and relish.

She could, he told her, keep one particular thing by courtesy of the Commander-in-Chief, the Duke of Cumberland. What was it to be? She suggested her store of tea. No, said Wolfe, tea was scarce in the Army and he was sure she couldn't have that. Chocolate, then? No; chocolate was scarce too.

I mentioned several other things, [she remembered] particularly my china. That he told me was, *a great deal of it*, very pretty, and they were very fond of china themselves; but as they had no ladies travelled with them, I might perhaps have *some of it*. I then desired to have my pictures. He said he supposed I could not wish to have *them all*. I replied that I did not pretend to name any, except my son's. He asked me if I had a son, where was he? I said I had sent him into the country to make room for them. . . . He asked, how old my son was. I said, about fourteen. Said he, then he is not a child, and you will have to produce him; and thus we parted.

The next day Major Wolfe came back to see her again and told her that the Duke had received a petition which she had addressed to him and had consequently decided that she could keep everything after all. But when she sent to the house for anything she was told she could not have it. She asked for 'a pair of breeches for my son'; but her request was refused. Then she asked for 'a little tea for myself, for a bottle of ale, for some flour to make bread'. But each time she was told she could not have whatever it was she had asked for. At length Wolfe brought out the picture of her son and told her she could have that, but not its frame, which was 'a gilt one and very handsome', as the General wanted it. What the General wanted it for, Wolfe did not say. Mrs Gordon found it left behind in the house when the English officers had gone.

The rude and unsympathetic young major seemed anxious to prove that despite his smooth, pale skin, his silk-like hair and somewhat effeminate face, he was no milksop. Writing to a friend of the family he described a massacre of rebels with evident satisfaction. The cavalry charge, he wrote, was 'done with wonderful spirit, and completed the victory with much slaughter. . . . The rebels, besides their natural inclinations, had orders not to give quarter to our men. We had an opportunity of avenging ourselves for that and many other things, and indeed we did not neglect it. As few Highlanders were made prisoners as possible.'

His contemptuous dislike of the Highlanders, and indeed of all Scotsmen, was extreme. He told Captain Rickson,

6

one of his few intimate friends that Sir Humphrey Bland, the Commander-in-Chief in Scotland, was 'doting' and that if he could have had his way, M'Pherson, Lord Lovat's son-in-law and a notorious rebel, would be sought out by two hundred men 'with orders to massacre the whole clan if they shew the least symptoms of rebellion'. He had tried, he said, to capture M'Pherson himself. He had sent out a small detachment under the command of a sergeant with instructions to take the rebel, and to shoot him if it seemed at all likely that his clan would try to release him. This would result, he supposed with frank indifference, in the destruction of his whole detachment and would give him the 'excuse (without waiting for any instructions) to march into their country *où j'aurais fait main basse, sans miséricorde. . . .* It was my real intention,' he insisted as if Rickson could not have believed him capable of so Machiavellian a scheme. 'They are a people better governed by fear than favour.'

It was his misfortune to come back to these despised people after a short term of duty on the Continent, where he was wounded at Laufeldt and had the pleasure of being complimented on his bravery by the Duke of Cumberland.

His distinguished service in Flanders led to his being given command of the 20th Regiment on his return to Scotland, although he was not yet twenty-three. But he liked the regiment little better than the people among whom it was stationed. 'Few of my companions', he wrote to his mother from Glasgow, 'surpass me in common knowledge but most of them in vice.' The Scotch civilians were 'civil, designing and treacherous'; the women 'cold, coarse and cunning'. He looked upon himself 'as an exile. With respect to the inhabitants I am so', he complained. 'For I dislike 'em much.'

In their turn the officers of the regiment did not greatly care for the man and less for his régime. Wolfe worked them hard and long. When their attitude gave eloquent testimony of their resentment they were told that an officer 'should not think he does too much'. Certainly their commanding officer never thought that he did too much himself. Hard as his officers worked, he worked twice as hard as any of them. He refused leave and rarely left the regimental lines. Lord George Sackville, the Colonel of the regiment, who admired his dedicated application to his duty, suggested that he really ought to get some leave, but Wolfe would not consent 'even to his asking'. Sackville was concerned about his future. He was quite the most remarkable officer in the Army, but he had no social graces whatever and could not hope to get on in the Army as he should do, unless he knew how to behave elegantly in the best company and made an effort to become liked as well as respected by the 'heads of our trade', as Sackville disrespectfully referred to them.

The advice of the worldly-wise Lord George made an impression on Wolfe although he did not immediately take it. He was depressed and ill and could not be bothered with anything except his regimental duties, which, whatever his health or mood, were carried out with the strictest care. 'I who am far from being sprightly even in my gayity', he confessed in a letter written from Scotland at this time, 'am the very reverse of it now.'

And then in March 1750, on the recommendation of Lord George Sackville, who was at the time on terms of intimate friendship with the Duke of Cumberland, his long-awaited promotion to lieutenant-colonel was gazetted. Again Sackville advised him to soften his dedicated professionalism with more socially agreeable accomplishments. And now he began to try. His promotion appeared to have given him new heart and to have helped him overcome that constant, distressing readiness to take offence. He still had no charm and little capacity for small talk. His occasional jokes were painfully heavy. His long, awkward silences would suddenly be broken by a disconcerting flow of ill-ordered speech. But his face, not yet drawn by pain and illness into those white and bony, bird-like lines which were later to make it so curiously unattractive, was interestingly ascetic and could abruptly be transformed by a brief, refreshing smile; while his gaucheries now seemed almost attractive in a colonel so young and so obviously making an effort to be pleasant. Although not a distinguished dancer, women found his determination to become one appealing; and if he was not, nor ever became, a charming or even a likeable man, he was not a dull one either. He was beginning to come out of his military shell, to the surprise of at least one young lady who had previously written to his mother to complain of her son's neglect of her sex.

It did seem, however, that this new interest in women was more calculated than spontaneous. Women had helped other officers in their careers and they might perhaps help him.

Some time previously he had met and conceived a sudden and unexpected admiration for Miss Elizabeth Lawson, daughter of Sir Wilfred Lawson, who had been Member of Parliament for Cumberland, and niece of General Mordaunt, a senior officer with considerable influence at the Horse Guards. But it was a curiously half-hearted affair. She was—and he readily agreed that she was—a rather plain young woman, tall and thin like himself, with small features and a pear-shaped face and he never heard her name mentioned, he protested, 'without a twitch' and hardly ever 'thought of her with indifference'. He did not, however, press his suit very hard and she, growing tired of his indecision, decided not to marry him anyway. There were, she is reported to have said, without naming them, 'unsurmountable obstacles' to the match. Part of the trouble was that she only had £12,000, and his parents considered this wholly inadequate for a young man of his promise who had no fortune of his own. They strongly urged the charms and merits of a certain Miss Hoskins from Croydon, who had £30,000; and James, conscious as always of his filial duty and the fear of his mother's anger, gave in. He refused to consider Miss

9

Hoskins, but he agreed not to marry Miss Lawson. His capitulation, however, was attended by a sulky ill-temper, and he repeatedly reminded his mother of her harshness. It was his only attempt to question her authority, his one demonstration of independence. It was as if he subconsciously wished to find in her a scapegoat for his own inadequacy or impotence, an excuse for an inability to feel a normal sexual passion.

Certainly his enthusiasm did not last long, and as he confessed to his friend Captain Rickson he found it easy to forget the girl when he was parted from her. 'If I am kept long here', he wrote to him from Scotland, 'the fire will be extinguished. Young flames must be constantly fed or they'll evaporate.' He was, no doubt, thankful that his mother had given him some good excuse not to marry, for the idea itself did not appeal to him. 'There is a great probability I shall never marry', he said. 'I shall hardly engage in an affair of that nature purely for money, nor do I believe that my infatuation will ever be strong enough to persuade me that people cannot live without it.'

There seems indeed some reason for supposing that the disinclination might have had a deeper cause. There was much in his temperament suggestive of the latent homosexual. The suppression and sublimation of homosexual tendencies is undoubtedly a reasonable explanation for the neurosis which complicated his character. That they were suppressed seems certain. Although on one occasion apparently he was guilty of some unspecified indiscretion and in consequence received a letter in which his father criticized his behaviour and some of his friends. In a previously unpublished reply Wolfe admitted his stupidity and apologized for it. 'You very justly ridicule the situation I was in', he wrote. 'It was truly ridiculous.'

There are further hints—and they were never more than hints—in a few other letters, particularly in those written to his young subaltern, the exceptionally good-looking

Duke of Richmond. They are, of course, not evidence; but they add something to a likely supposition.

There is, on the other hand, no lack of evidence to shew that whatever the impulses were, no man or woman was or ever would be as important to Wolfe as his career. Everything must give way to that. Nothing which might help him get on must be left undone.

He had made up for a poor and brief education by diligent study and reading, but he was constantly disturbed by Sackville's contention that he would never reach the top of his profession without acquiring that polish and easy confidence in society which so steadfastly eluded him. His promotion to lieutenant-colonel at so early an age had given him confidence, but still he felt that he had much to learn. He would never learn it, he was sure, in Scotland, which he detested, nor even in London, which he found depressing and enervating. And so he decided to go to Paris.

The decision once made, he carried out his plan with accustomed thoroughness. He borrowed money from his parents, as he had often had to do in the past, and after some opposition from the new Colonel of his regiment set off with the professed intention of learning French, dancing, riding, and fencing. He never supposed that it might also prove an enjoyable holiday. It was as if he were going to school. And in Paris he lived a life of strict regularity. He arose early, attended his lessons punctually, rarely dined out, was usually in bed before eleven. Four or five days in the week he was 'up an hour before day (that is six hours before any other fine gentleman in Paris)'. 'I succeed much better', he wrote home, 'in fencing and riding than I do in the art of dancing, for they suit my genius better; and I improve a little in the French language.' Once when he did go to a ball he was not greatly taken with the company he found there. Although the French ladies were 'well bred, delicate and genteel', they were also unfortunately 'a little inclined to gluttony' and 'troubled with frequent indigestion'. The men had 'good faces and fine hair', but had 'bad limbs' and were 'ill-shaped'.

After having borrowed more money for an extended stay and further tuition, he was recalled to his regiment on the death of its acting commander and returned to England, satisfied with his progress.

He did not, however, find much opportunity or feel much inclination to make use of his new accomplishments. The regiment had gone slack in his absence, and he himself was far from well. He nearly fainted one day when an officer had a fit in the mess, and his letters were fuller than ever of hypochondriacal comments on his health and medicinal recommendations to his mother. The officers and men were lazier even than before. 'If I stay much longer in the regiment', he protested, 'I shall be perfectly corrupt. The officers are loose and profligate, and the soldiers are very devils.' In his efforts to reform them he once more gave up all social activities and advised his officers to do the same, much to the annoyance of at least one bright young girl who had never known such a dull lot of men in the usually gay garrison. She was quite out of conceit, she complained, with the 'bookish Colonel' who was responsible for her boring evenings.

But Wolfe felt that he had more important work to do than entertain a band of arch and giggling girls, and he ignored them all and their mothers too. Within a few months his regiment was reckoned to be 'the best in the Army, so far as drill and discipline go'. And he was determined to make it remain so.

Once they had become, under his strict and conscientious surveillance, a proper unit again he encouraged the officers to go to balls and assemblies, for 'it softens their manners and makes 'em civil'. Willing to show them how vastly improved as a dancer he had himself become, he went with them. 'I commonly go along with them', he told his mother, 'to see how they conduct themselves. I am only afraid they should fall in love or marry. Whenever I perceive the symptoms, or anyone else makes the discovery, we fall upon the delinquent without mercy, till he grows out of conceit with the new passion. By this method we have broke through many amorous dalliances and dissolved many ties of eternal love and devotion. My experience in these matters', he added, harping back to his parents' opposition to Miss Lawson, which they were never allowed to forget, 'helps me to find out my neighbour's weakness and furnishes me with arms to oppose his folly.'

Balls and assemblies were, however, all very well, he complained, but they did not teach his officers anything about war. And having made his regiment the best in the Army, Wolfe was impatient to use it. As the months of inactivity went slowly by, his anxiety to fight became desperate and made him restless and ill-tempered again.

Nothing seemed to be happening. After several wasted years in Scotland and now three more in Kent and the south of England, he felt he was in a rut and being forgotten. He was still almost the youngest lieutenant-colonel in the Army, but that was not enough. When Lieutenant-Colonel Honeywood, a man of considerable influence and wealth, was given the colonelcy of the regiment, he threatened to retire. Although Honeywood was very much his senior Wolfe took the appointment as a personal insult. 'Colonel Honeywood's being put to this regiment is no compliment to me,' he indignantly told his father, who was now a major-general and had been doing his best to use what little influence he possessed on his touchy son's behalf. Eighteen months later, when his desire for a colonelcy had become almost pathological in its intensity, Wolfe warned that if 'any soldier is preferred when my turn comes, I shall acquaint the Secretary of War that I am sensible of the injury that is done me, and will take the earliest opportunity to put it out of his or any man's power to repeat it'. In September 1757 he was considering taking the offered

13

appointment of Quartermaster-General in Ireland. It was not a suitable post for an ambitious soldier, but it was at least one way of obtaining his longed-for promotion. He made it clear, however, that he would 'certainly not go to Ireland without the rank of colonel'.

And then, in the depths of his despair, he was saved from being forgotten in Ireland by a sudden and unexpected chance to make his reputation. He was appointed Quartermaster-General in the expedition about to sail to raid the French coast at Rochefort under command of General Mordaunt whom, as Elizabeth Lawson's uncle, he had frequently met. It seemed a godsent opportunity. He prepared for the expedition with enthusiasm, considered every possible means of attack, spent hours poring over maps of the coastline behind Ile de Ré and Oléron as he looked for likely landing-places on the jagged shore.

The expedition was a fiasco. Neither the military nor the naval commander seemed able to make up his mind whether or not to attack. And when Wolfe asked and obtained permission to reconnoitre the shore and prepared a report advocating action, his superiors considered it impracticable and gave the order to retire.

Only Wolfe and Richard Howe, then a young naval officer, escaped criticism at the subsequent enquiry. Wolfe indeed hurled his reproofs at everyone connected with the enterprise except the brave and taciturn Howe with whom he had 'contracted a friendship', which Walpole described as being like 'the union of a cannon and gunpowder'.

'The true state of the case is', Wolfe told his Uncle Walter in a letter of angry disdain, 'that our sea officers do not care to be engaged in any business of this sort, when little is to be had but blows and reputation ; and the officers of the infantry are so profoundly ignorant, that an enterprise of any vigour astonishes them to that degree that they have not strength of mind nor confidence to carry it through.' He dismissed with contempt the defence that an assault on

Rochefort would have resulted in heavy loss of life. 'In particular circumstances and times', he believed, 'the loss of a thousand men is rather advantageous to a nation than otherwise.'

Less than three months later, however, he was given another opportunity and was able to forget his disappointment and anger in preparing for an expedition of far greater scope and importance.

He had written to Pitt, offering his services and, in his own phrase, had thrown himself in the way of the American war. Pitt, who had heard good reports of the zealous and energetic young officer and had noted his conduct at Rochefort, accepted his offer and gave him the opportunity he wanted of fighting in the New World.

As soon as he knew that he had been chosen for the American expedition, he took the trouble with his usual care and thoroughness to learn all he could of American tactics and American history.

Ever since the end of the sixteenth century, relations between the English and French in North America had been growing worse. In the south of the vast and silent continent the Spanish and Portuguese had found sugar and gold, while in the north the French and English had discovered two things less romantic but no less valuable— codfish and furs. And it was principally upon these two commodities that French power in Canada was founded and about which the quarrels began.

At first the New World meant no more to France than a collection of trading posts and fishing stations, and it was not until Samuel de Champlain, a nautical surveyor of great energy and talent, sailed up the St Lawrence River on a voyage of exploration in 1603 that a Frenchman saw in the immense and trackless wilderness that stretched beyond the river banks, the heart of a new empire.

Champlain realized, as the aboriginal Iroquois Indians

had done before him, that the St Lawrence River was the key to Canada, the one safe, easy route to the interior. In 1608 he built a post at a point where the river narrowed and an island made a natural anchorage. It was known to the Iroquois as Quebec—'the shut-in place'; and it became the most important post in Canada. Even after the foundation of Montreal farther upstream in 1642, Quebec remained the real and undisputed capital of New France, and the 150 miles of river between the two towns was the only part of the whole of North America where Frenchmen were to settle in any density, and so became the inevitable battleground where the fate of Canada was to be decided.

The first traders and settlers were mainly Huguenots, but after the murder of Henry IV in 1610 the revival of Catholicism and religious enthusiasm in France spread to Canada, and Jesuit missionaries came out with every expedition and became an essential part of Canadian life. As French trading posts in the seventeenth century extended farther and farther south, past the area of the Great Lakes and down the Mississippi Valley towards the Gulf of Mexico, the missionaries and priests, under the vigilant direction of Laval, the fiery, puritanical Bishop of Quebec, moved about by canoe and in the saddle, riding, paddling, and walking for hundreds of miles between trading post and settlement, keeping alive the word of God in the hearts of the faithful and bringing, with less success, the heathen Indians into the Christian fold.

The English attitude to colonization and conquest was quite different. They had not come to convert the heathen, but to make money. Although they cultivated the Iroquois tribes, whom the French had fought for possession of the St Lawrence River, and in particular the Mohawks, the English did not seek to collaborate with the Indians but to drive them farther west; and if they would not go, to kill them. They endeavoured to become settled fishermen and farmers in ever growing but compact communities. While the French were constantly spreading themselves in isolated groups over a vast terrain, the English concentrated on the expansion of settled farmships and fishing communities which became in time villages, towns, and ports, mainly along the Atlantic seaboard between New England and Georgia, east of the Appalachian Mountains.

By these means and by a constant and increasing flow of immigrants from Britain their settlements grew and prospered. By 1750 the number of British in America was nearly a million, while the French, dotted about over thousands of square miles behind the Appalachian Mountains and to the north in Canada, numbered less than eighty thousand, despite their remarkable fertility.

By now the war between France and England in Europe had spread to America. Already the mutual jealousies, the religious prejudices, and the fierce rivalry for the Indian trade had led to frequent raids of Iroquois Indians, drunk with English rum, on French outposts and to the retaliatory attacks of supposedly Catholic Indians fired with French brandy on English settlements. But towards the middle of the eighteenth century the war began in earnest.

The French, determined to keep the English confined between the Appalachian Mountains and the sea, began to consider the building of a chain of forts to link Quebec with Louisiana, and they sent an expedition down the Ohio Valley to claim it for Louis XV. Although the expedition did little more than plant lead tablets at strategic points, where the Indians found them and immediately melted them down for bullets, Robert Dinwiddie, the Governor of Virginia, decided to reply to the threat, and sent the twenty-one-year-old Major George Washington to build a British fort at the junction of the Allegheny and Monongahela Rivers. But Washington's small force was outnumbered by the French at a trading station known as The Great Meadows and forced to surrender. The French were able to complete the building of a fort, which they had already started, on the site selected by Washington. They christened it Fort Duquesne. It was later to become better known as Pittsburgh.

In the following year General Braddock, a fierce, red-faced soldier of some talent but little imagination, came over from England and in June 1755 set out from Virginia to capture the new French fort. But on 9 July, the day before he expected to reach it, Braddock was ambushed, and his heavy-footed English regiments were massacred by Indians in the forests by the banks of the Monongahela River.

Concerned at the turn of events in America, the British Government in London decided that a more determined effort must be made to give the French a lesson and sent out the Earl of Loudon as Commander-in-Chief in America. But Loudon was an even less imaginative general than Braddock and had none of his courage. He was indeed, as Walpole disdainfully put it, a commander whom 'a child might outwit or terrify with a pop-gun'. And while he was laboriously making preparations, the Marquis de Montcalm, the recently appointed French Commander-in-Chief, swept down from Fort Ticonderoga and captured the English fort at William Henry.

It was against this background of British stupidity and defeat that Pitt had had to consider the operations for 1758.

In discussions with Lord Ligonier, the clever old soldier who had now succeeded the Duke of Cumberland as Commander-in-Chief, and Lord Anson the First Lord of the Admiralty, Pitt had realized immediately that the continent's geography severely limited the lines of attack. Owing to impenetrable forests, wide and fast-flowing rivers, and long mountain ranges there were only three routes along which armies could successfully manœuvre and fight. One of these lines ran north-west from Virginia across the valleys in the Pennsylvania mountains; a second ran west from Albany along the River Mohawk to Lake Ontario; the best ran due north from New York towards the St Lawrence

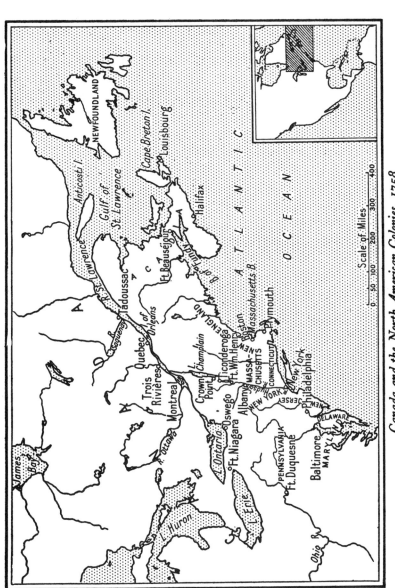

Canada and the North American Colonies, 1758

River. Previously the principal operations had started in Virginia, and the British had advanced against the French from the south. Pitt and his advisers thought a more successful assault could be made by an amphibious attack from the north down the wide St Lawrence River, and it was upon this route to the Canadian interior that they concentrated their attention.

2

Towards the northern end of Cape Breton Island in Nova Scotia, at the mouth of the Gulf of St Lawrence, stood a lonely fortress commanding the route to Quebec and Montreal and the heart of French-occupied Canada. It was called Louisbourg and stood isolated and forbidding at the edge of a jagged coast-line, looking out across the bitter sea. Most of its four thousand inhabitants were there because it was the strongest fortified garrison on the Western Atlantic coast, the 'Dunkirk of the North', the 'bulwark of Canada'. Even the few fishermen and priests who lived there were expected in times of emergency to go to the help of the three thousand troops behind the rock-like ramparts and to assist if necessary in the firing of the four hundred cannon whose muzzles showed menacing and silent in every embrasure.

The French had built Louisbourg shortly after the Treaty of Utrecht in 1713 and had fortified it at a cost of more than a million pounds. In 1745, when France and England were at war again, the colonists of New England under William Shirley, Governor of Massachusetts, had, with the assistance of Admiral Warren and a small British fleet, unexpectedly captured the fortress after a spirited five weeks' siege. Three years later, to the anger of the British colonists in America, Louisbourg had been returned to France at the Treaty of Aix-la-Chapelle, and the French, realizing its importance and having been prepared to make considerable concessions at Aix-la-Chapelle in order to regain it, now spent enormous sums on improving its defences. In 1758 the French and Canadians were satisfied that it was as well defended and as strong as it could reasonably be made.

At the beginning of the year Pitt decided that, before any serious operations to drive the French out of Canada could be put in hand, Louisbourg must be taken. On Lord Ligonier's recommendation he recalled Colonel Jeffrey Amherst from Germany, promoted him, and gave him command of the expedition which was to be taken across the Atlantic by Admiral Boscawen. Pitt appointed three brigadiers to go with Amherst. Two of them, Lawrence and Whitmore, were men of proved ability who had already had experience of fighting in America. The third was James Wolfe.

Wolfe's capabilities as a senior commander were, of course, as yet unknown; but Lord George Sackville, who was now Lieutenant-General of Ordnance, always spoke highly of him, and Ligonier and Pitt were willing to give the keen young man a chance. Wolfe accepted the challenge with enthusiasm and pleasure. He would make a name for himself this time or die in the attempt. 'All I wish for myself', he told his mother on 17 January, 'is that I may at all times be ready and firm to meet that fate we cannot shun and to die gracefully and properly when the hour comes.' On the same day he wrote to Rickson and again mentioned the possibility of death. 'Being of the profession of arms', he said, 'I would seek all occasions to serve and therefore have thrown myself in the way of the American war; though I know that the very passage threatens my life, and that my constitution must be utterly ruined and undone.'

While waiting at Portsmouth for the weather to improve, his melancholy increased and he grew impatient and irritable.

'The condition of the troops that compose this garrison', he wrote to Lord George Sackville in disgust, '(or rather vagabonds that stroll about in dirty red clothes from one gin shop to another) exceeds all belief. There is not the least shadow of discipline, care or attention.'

'The want of company and of amusement', he complained

to his mother, 'can be supplied with books and exercise, but the necessity of living in the midst of the diabolical citizens of Portsmouth is a real and unavoidable calamity. It is a doubt to me if there is another such collection of demons upon the whole earth. . . . I should be glad if we were at sea, though we have no very agreeable prospect before me; however', he ended on a familiar note of self-congratulatory confidence, 'I hope to overcome that and if not have a mind strong enough to endure that and still severer trials.'

The passage across the Atlantic was quite as bad as Wolfe had feared. Although he sailed out of the Solent on 19 February, he did not see the rugged coast-line of Nova Scotia until 9 May. For nearly three months he had been tossed and rolled, appallingly seasick, in his cramped quarters and endured one of the worst Atlantic crossings that even the most experienced of the sailors could remember.

Although extremely weak he insisted on accompanying the other commanders on 2 June on a reconnaissance of the Louisbourg shore. The seas were rough and the rowing-boats in which Amherst and the brigadiers sat, with tele-scopes held to their eyes, swayed dizzily.

It was decided that Lawrence and Whitmore should make a feint of attacking the two coves close to the town, while Wolfe should make the real attack at the cove of Le Coromandière about four miles from Louisbourg Harbour in Gabarus Bay. But owing to wind and fog it was six days before the assault could be made. At dawn on 8 June the guns of the whole fleet opened up and in a blaze of thunder-ing fire the landing-boats were rowed towards the shore.

As Wolfe's brigade approached Le Coromandière, the ships' gunners held their fire for fear of dropping a shell short amidst the shoal of landing-craft. The boats, packed with red-coated soldiers, bobbed slowly towards the rocky shore in the sudden silence, while the twelve hundred

Frenchmen defending that part of the coast watched and waited for the order to fire, secure behind a deep abattis of felled pine-trees.

When the order came the landing-craft were so close inshore that the French could see the English sailors' pigtails, and hear the sound of the soldiers' voices as they shouted good-natured insults to each other across the water. The French gunners had held their fire to good purpose, for now the effect of the battery of guns opening up in an instantaneous cannonade was devastating. In showers of spray and plumes of smoke, boats splintered and upturned and men were hurled into the sea, where they floundered helplessly in their heavy uniforms. Sailors holding out oars and throwing ropes to the spluttering, choking soldiers, were peppered by French sharpshooters as they tried to pull them back on board and were washed off their feet by sudden rushes of cascading water thrown up by exploding shells. Wolfe, the flagstaff of his boat shot away, gave the order to sheer off, believing it impossible to get ashore. Three boats, however, instead of turning off altered course slightly and kept on. The subalterns in command of them had seen a place, protected by a ledge of rock from the batteries on the cliff above, where it seemed they might be able to land, and ignoring Wolfe's order they made straight for it. Within a minute or two the boats had raced forward over the surf and the young officers had jumped out on to the rocks followed by their men.

Wolfe, shown the way in, was quick to follow. Countermanding his previous signal, he ordered the other boats to make for the same spot and on reaching it he leapt out on to the rocks, waving his cane in the air and shouting encouragement and advice to the men behind him. Not all the boats were lucky. Some were dashed on to the rocks and splitting their sides sank in an instant, while others, upturned in the swelling sea, buffeted each other like twigs in a millrace. A hundred men were drowned.

But the others raced inland. Their uniforms were soaked, their muskets and powder were sodden, but, brandishing their bayonets as the only effective weapon most of them had, they presented a frightening spectacle. The French defenders, surprised by this abrupt and alarming change in fortune and seeing the English reinforcements already approaching the shore, decided to retreat to the walls of Louisbourg. The invaders had triumphed.

Hopes of an early reduction of Louisbourg itself, however, were soon dispelled. For nine days the troops waited on a wide front some two miles to the south of the town for the siege guns to be landed. The days were spent in improving their entrenchments and blockhouses, the nights in fear of attack by bands of Micmac Indians. The weather was appalling and the heavy grey seas roared and thundered with depressing tautophony on the black rocks below.

Wolfe thought the whole conduct of the siege 'exceeding slow and injudicious' and the landing to have been 'rash and ill-advised'. Amherst, who had been trained in Germany where fortresses were slowly and deliberately starved and battered into surrender, was, he considered, unnecessarily cautious. Major Mackellar, who had succeeded the stupid Colonel Bastide as Chief Engineer, was incompetent. His fellow-brigadier, Whitmore, was a 'poor, old, sleepy man'. The American rangers he dismissed, using a favourite word, as 'canaille'. The Americans, in fact, were 'in general', he told Lord George Sackville with extravagant and unjustified contempt, 'the dirtiest, most contemptible, cowardly dogs that you can conceive. There is no depending on them in action. They fall down dead in their own dirt and desert by battalions, officers and all.'

He gained credit for himself in the operations by the subsequently much publicized use of the light infantry under his command, who, advancing in small parties and in loose formation, skirmished with the enemy and then immediately retreated. These tactics had been devised by the brilliant Swiss officer Colonel Bouquet of the 60th Regiment (usually known as the Royal Americans), who had been trained in Indian fighting by the enterprising American ranger Robert Rogers. Their merits had already been recognized by Lord Howe, whose own soldiers in the 55th Regiment had practised them successfully in previous campaigns. To the experienced American ranger there was nothing new about them. They were indeed the only possible method of fighting Indians, who respected no ordinary rules of warfare. They were found to be quite as effective against the French, and Wolfe consequently received much praise for using them.

One of his officers, a rather learned and ingratiating young man, told him that they reminded him of Xenophon's description of the καρδοῦχοι who had harassed his rear when he had retreated over mountain ranges. 'I had it from Xenophon', Wolfe replied tartly although in the circumstances it seemed most unlikely that he had. 'But our friends here are astonished at what I have done, because they have read nothing.'

Apart from these lightning forays by the light infantry the operations were dull and hard going. The besieging army crawled slowly and laboriously forward over the barren, rocky ground and through the pools of soggy mud towards the ramparts of Louisbourg, behind which the French guns thundered ceaselessly. As the soldiers pushed closer towards the walls of the fortress, enemy detachments crept out in the darkness and fell upon them as they struggled forward, tired and sweating, silently cursing the heavy guns which stuck and slithered in the mud.

The French troops, fresh from rest in their comparatively comfortable quarters in Louisbourg, slashed and lunged at the besieging troops, who fought back with desperate anger. In one of these hand-to-hand affrays Wolfe, who had recently returned from the other side of Louisbourg, where he had skilfully established a battery at Lighthouse Point, gave further evidence of his remarkable personal courage and surprised a soldier of the 60th by appearing to be actually enjoying the furious and bloody engagement.

Bombarded from their right by French ships lying at anchor in the west of the harbour and harried on their left by the sudden raids of screeching Indians, the British were unable until the middle of July to get the siege guns into positions from which they could deliver a damaging fire against the fortress. But during the last two weeks of the month, as the men entrenched themselves in a zigzag line, which in places was less than three hundred yards from the walls of the town, the cannonade from their hundred heavy siege guns was constant and devastating.

Throughout the days and the moonlit nights the heavy pieces roared at the town. Behind the walls fires broke out frequently and scores of wooden houses tumbled in flames ; sailors and fishermen and hundreds of townspeople, women as well as men, came to the help of the exhausted gunners on the ramparts ; and the sick and wounded were huddled together in the rapidly diminishing places of shelter. Towards the end of the month great cracks appeared in the masonry of the walls and the ramparts began to crumble. The Governor sent a plea to Amherst for a cease-fire while he evacuated the wounded and the women and children. Amherst told Wolfe of the request and the sternly unsympathetic young brigadier replied with scorn that 'when the French are in a scrape, they are ready to cry out on behalf of the human species ; when fortune favours them, none more bloody or more inhuman. Montcalm has changed the very nature of war, and has forced us, in some measure, to a deterring and dreadful vengeance.'

On 26 July, after almost a month of brave but increasingly hopeless defiance, a French officer came out of the ruined fortress with a white flag of surrender. He was told that the English would only accept unconditional surrender within the hour. The French immediately rejected the

27

offer and prepared for a stand to the death, but the citizens prevailed upon them not to sacrifice their lives in the selfish cause of military honour, and the next day the dejected troops ambled out of Louisbourg and sulkily flung down their arms.

The passage to the St Lawrence River was now open, and Wolfe anxiously awaited orders to press on to Quebec. But the orders never came. Instead Amherst was sent to New York to the help of General Abercromby, the incompetent Earl of Loudon's quite as incompetent successor, who had lost nearly two thousand men in a suicidal attack on the French fort at Ticonderoga and had retreated to his base on Lake George. Whitmore was left in Louisbourg and Wolfe was ordered to ravage the Canadian settlements along the coast of the Gulf of St Lawrence. It was not an operation which required any military skill or provided much excitement, but he had confessed to Lord George Sackville on 30 July that it would give him 'pleasure to see the Canadian vermin sacked and pillaged', and so the duty to carry out the punishment on those 'hell-hounds' cannot have been so distasteful as it would have been if he had had to carry it out upon a people for whom he felt less hate. Certainly he performed it with his usual notable thoroughness.

As soon as the operation was completed he returned home to England, without waiting for any specific instructions from London to do so. When he did ultimately receive his instructions and found that they required him to remain in Halifax under Brigadier Lawrence he flew into a rage, although they were by then almost a year out of date, having followed him twice across the Atlantic. Though he acknowledged Lawrence to be 'a very worthy man' (he was also several years older and his senior as brigadier) he would not submit to such indignity. 'I would certainly have desired leave to resign my commission', he told the Ministry. 'For as I neither ask nor expect any favour, so I never intend to submit to any ill usage whatever.'

3

THE crossing of the Atlantic was once more a terrible ordeal. He reached Portsmouth on 1 November, 1758, ill, exhausted, and depressed. The capture of Louisbourg had been almost forgotten by now in England, and Wolfe went to join the 2nd Battalion of the 20th Regiment in Salisbury.

He did not attempt to conceal his opinion of the way the operations in America had been and were being conducted. 'Our attempt to land where we did', he wrote, 'was rash and injudicious, our success unexpected (by me) and undeserved. There was no prodigious exertion of courage in the affair; an officer and thirty men would have made it impossible to get ashore where we did. Our proceedings in other respects are as slow and tedious as this undertaking was ill-advised and desperate.' But if service in America had been unrewarding, service at home was a great deal worse. After only four weeks in England he had had enough of his fellow-officers. He had never liked mess life and now he liked it less than ever. He was anxious to be on the move again towards another battle. At the beginning of December he wrote to Pitt again and offered his services, 'particularly in the River St Lawrence if any operations are to be carried on there'. 'I have this day signified to Mr Pitt', he told Rickson, 'that he may dispose of my slight carcass as he pleases. . . . I am in a very bad condition both with the gravel and rheumatism but I had much rather die than decline any kind of service that offers.'

Before writing to Pitt he had twice written to Ligonier. In his first letter he had asked for permission to go to

London with a view to a discussion about his future. Receiving no immediate reply he wrote again; this time adding a request for an appointment in Germany. But Ligonier had not been encouraging and the rather cool tone of his reply had increased Wolfe's depression.

This depression, he thought, was due largely to his pitiable health and he obtained leave from the 20th in order to take the waters at Bath and to prepare himself for any future exertions which he might be called upon to make. Slowly during December he began to get better and with the improvement in his health came brighter spirits. He spoke of the forthcoming campaign in America as if it were already arranged that he should go on it. On occasions he was almost gay, although, as he had himself confessed, he was never sprightly even in his gaiety.

One day in a mood of unaccustomed sentiment he asked Miss Catherine Lowther to marry him and she accepted his offer, although in view of his expected departure for America no plans for the marriage were made. She was the sister of Sir James Lowther, an immensely wealthy and excessively unpopular Member of Parliament who was, so Alexander Carlyle said, 'more detested than any man alive . . . truly a madman, though too rich to be confined', and who according to Walpole was 'equally unamiable in public and private'. His sister had a long, sharp face with a thin nose and dimpled chin and she might have been rather plain had it not been for her lovely eyes. Little is known of her character. She was said to be ambitious and was generally considered to be kind and somewhat stupid.

Soon after Christmas the anxiously awaited news came. Wolfe was told he had been assigned a part in the impending operations and was called to Pitt's country-house near London to discuss them. He left immediately.

The Ministry's plan, he learned, was simple enough. There were that spring to be two main attacks on the French in Canada: one from the north, the other from the south.

Jeffrey Amherst, Lord Ligonier's protégé, was to attack from the south and to take the French fort at Ticonderoga, where Abercromby had been so cruelly beaten the year before, and then advance up Lake Champlain towards Montreal; while a second amphibious army was to be sent from the north up the St Lawrence River to attack Quebec. If all went well with Amherst he might advance still farther north and at the same time consider the advisability of a third drive westwards from Massachusetts along the route of the Mohawk River to clear the French from the banks of Lake Ontario and capture Niagara. If all three attacks succeeded, there could be no doubt that French power in Canada would be finished.

The most important, crucial, and dramatic of the attacks was the sweep from the north up the St Lawrence River to Quebec. It was this one which was to be entrusted to Wolfe. He would be given, Pitt told him, every opportunity to succeed. Admiral Saunders, who had accompanied Anson on his famous voyage round the world in the *Centurion* and was one of the ablest officers in the Navy—for it was essentially an amphibious operation—would command the fleet, which was to be a large one; Wolfe would be promoted to major-general; he could have £500 for expenses in addition to a major-general's pay of £14 a week; and as for the officers under his command he could, within reason, have whom he wanted. Although Amherst was to have supreme command in America, it was understood that Wolfe was to have a free hand at Quebec.

Here at last was the opportunity he had been waiting for—an army to command, a campaign to organize, an enemy to defeat!

His excitement and pleasure were undisguised. He had, he said, with a sudden access of unusual modesty, been given a 'greater part' than he 'wished or desired. The backwardness of some of the older officers has in some measure forced the Government to come down so low. I shall do my best. . . . If I have health and constitution enough for the campaign, I shall think myself a lucky man ; what happens afterwards is of no great consequence.'

All day long during that cold January he made plans and wrote letters, consulted maps and manuals, drew sketches and diagrams. He studied the French despatches filched by Harry Paulet, the master of a small English merchant vessel, who had been held prisoner in Quebec the year before. Paulet had seen the despatches in the cabin of the ship in which he was being taken to France and had slipped overboard with them held between his teeth as the ship put into Vigo. He had been sent from Lisbon to London and had brought home with him not only the despatches but much useful information on Quebec and the navigation of the St Lawrence River.

Wolfe rarely thought of anything now except the conquest of Canada and the chance of fame, perhaps of immortality. 'Those who perish in their duty', he wrote with more than a breath of hope behind the sentiment, 'and in the service of their country, die honourably.'

In this excited mood, Wolfe was not prepared to brook any modification of Pitt's promise that he could choose his own officers. When he mentioned a name which did not altogether please the Commander-in-Chief, he bluntly told Ligonier that unless he had the 'assistance of such officers as I should name to him he would do me a great kindness to appoint some other person to the chief direction. This I fear was not understood as it deserved to be and people think it civil to doubt our sincerity sometimes in matters where it is most our interest to deal plainly.'

Eventually, however, the importunate brigadier was obliged to reach a compromise with the patient, courteous field-marshal. Subject to the approval of the Ministry, Wolfe could select two of the three brigadiers who were to accompany him. The choice of the third was to remain with the Ministry. For his part Wolfe selected Robert Monckton and James Murray.

The Hon. Robert Monckton, a son of Viscount Galway and a grandson of the Duke of Rutland, was the senior of the three. He was already in America as Colonel of the second battalion of the 60th Regiment and was anxiously awaiting the opportunity to serve in the forthcoming campaign. He had been cooped up in Halifax during the siege of Louisbourg and was impatient to prove his worth. He was six months older than Wolfe and had been commissioned at about the same time into the 3rd Regiment of Foot Guards, but after distinguished service in Flanders, where Wolfe had first met him, he seemed to have been forgotten. His pleasant, easy-going, guileless, and somewhat diffident nature was perhaps largely to blame for this apparent neglect and was also no doubt what made it possible for Wolfe to like him and to find in him no trace of that implicit jealousy which he was so quick to discover in so many other officers of his acquaintance. Monckton had a soft, kind face, a double chin and heavy-lidded eyes. Wolfe felt confident that he would do as he was told.

James Murray might prove more difficult. He was hard-working, ambitious and astute, as determined to achieve fame and glory as Wolfe himself. He had a vital little face with large eyes and an angular brow, a long, sharp nose, and Punch-like chin. But he was a capable officer and Wolfe knew that he also would carry out his orders to the letter. He had been born in 1725, the fifth son of the fourth Lord Elibank, and he had little money or influence. He had had long and almost continuous service abroad in the 15th Regiment and had purchased its command in 1751. His conduct at the siege of Louisbourg had been exemplary; and while Wolfe had criticized almost everyone else connected with it, for Murray he had had a word of praise. 'The public', he had told Lord George Sackville in a rare moment of respect, 'is much indebted to him.'

The third brigadier, the Hon. George Townshend, was quite a different personality from either of the other two, and Wolfe accepted him at the Commander-in-Chief's wish without enthusiasm. He was somewhat older than the others and had a less military background. He was the eldest son of the third Viscount Townshend and had been a lieutenant-colonel in the 1st Regiment of Foot Guards at the age of twenty-four. But a quarrel with the Duke of Cumberland had led to his retirement two years later. On the resignation of the Duke, however, he had decided to return to the Army and was promoted colonel in 1758. He had written to Pitt asking to be remembered if any suitable appointments on active service were available. He had no experience of commanding a battalion in the field, let alone a brigade; but as a subaltern at Culloden and Laufeldt he had proved that he was not as indolent and languid as he appeared to be. His coolness in battle was, indeed, proverbial. At Laufeldt he was watching an attack with several other members of the Duke of Cumberland's staff when a shell exploded near-by and blew off a German officer's head, the contents of which were spattered over his coat. 'I never knew before', he commented calmly, dabbing at his chest with a handker-chief, 'that Scheiger had so many brains.' Apart from any personal qualifications he might have had, the Townshends were, of course, a very important and influential family, and his late grandfather had been the Duke of Newcastle's brother-in-law. He was accordingly promoted brigadier, senior to Murray but junior to Monckton. The unselfishness of his agreement to serve under an officer younger than himself and his social inferior, and on an unfashionable colonial front was grudgingly applauded.

He was clever, aloof, quarrelsome, unlikeable, a little pompous, maliciously witty. Walpole, who heartily dis-liked both the man and his family, said that he was of a 'proud and sullen and contemptuous temper' and that so far as wrong-headedness went he was 'very proper for a hero'.

In a rather florid, Hanoverian way he was good-looking, although the fleshy chin and heavy pouches under his shrewd and mocking eyes gave the impression of a character at once worldly, self-indulgent, and sensual. He was happily married and had three children. He had much talent as an artist, and the caricatures, cruel and outrageously vulgar, which he drew of his friends and enemies had more than once resulted in a serious quarrel. From the first Wolfe disliked and distrusted him, but with an eye to the future wrote him a polite letter on 6 January in which he assured him that he had told Lord Ligonier when his name had been mentioned that 'what might be wanting in experience was amply made up, in an extent of capacity and activity of mind, that would find nothing difficult in our business'.

With the choice of the officers for his staff Wolfe was more happy. He would have liked as Quarter-Master-General either Rickson or his childhood friend George Warde. But Rickson was not available and Warde was posted to Germany. Colonel Guy Carleton, a thirty-five-year-old Irishman who was eventually selected for the appointment, was, however, also a friend of his and was, like Murray, one of those very few officers who had in Wolfe's opinion behaved well at Louisbourg, where he had commanded the 72nd Regiment.

The King, who disliked Carleton, not least because of some excessively impolite remarks concerning Hanoverian troops which he was said to have made, at first refused to sign his commission. Wolfe complained to Pitt and Pitt told Ligonier that as he had promised Wolfe the choice of his officers it was his duty as Commander-in-Chief to persuade the King to sign. Ligonier then tried again, but the King, who respected the gallant and weather-beaten old soldier and generally took his advice, was on this occasion adamant. Well, tell him, then, Pitt advised Ligonier, that 'in order to render any general completely responsible for his conduct, he should be made, as far as possible, inexcusable if he should fail; and that, consequently, whatever an officer entrusted with a service requests should be complied with'. This was an argument more acceptable to the King, and Carleton's commission was signed.

The appointment of Adjutant-General was also filled by an Irishman, Major Isaac Barré, the son of a French refugee who lived in Dublin. He was a big, ill-mannered, swarthy man who had first come to Wolfe's notice when he had applied to join his regiment at the time of the expedition to Rochefort.

As aides-de-camp Wolfe selected two young officers, Hervey Smith and Thomas Bell, both of whom admired him to the point of veneration. The officer appointed to command the artillery, which was to play an important part in the siege, was Colonel Williamson. The Chief Engineer, despite Wolfe's criticism of his conduct at Louisbourg, was to be Major Patrick Mackellar, who knew more about the problems of fortification in America than any other responsible engineer in the Army and who had been a prisoner of war in Quebec. Aged forty-two, he was one of the oldest men in Wolfe's entire army.

The extreme youthfulness of the senior officers, indeed, alarmed the King almost as much as it did the Duke of Newcastle. Angry complaints were received from officers and families who felt themselves slighted. As a concession to this ill-feeling it was decided that Wolfe should hold the rank of major-general only while in America. His commission was signed on 12 January.

But it was not for another month that all arrangements had been made and the expedition was ready to sail. The army was to number twelve thousand men, mainly drawn from American garrisons and ordered to await the arrival of the others in Louisbourg.

The evening before he was due to leave London for

Portsmouth, Wolfe was asked to dinner by Pitt. The other guest was Lord Temple, Pitt's brother-in-law. According to Temple, Wolfe's behaviour at this dinner was extremely curious. Towards the end of the meal the young general stood up and with shining eyes drew his sword and rapped it on the table. He then walked round the room, flourishing his sword in the air and delivering himself of the most extravagant boasts and threats. Pitt and Temple watched him in amazement and in painfully embarrassed silence. When the bluster of heroics died down, Pitt and Temple stood up and Wolfe with scarcely another word to either of them took his leave. 'Good God!' said Pitt when he had gone. 'That I should have entrusted the fate of the country and of the Administration to such hands!'

He was not drunk, Temple thought, because he 'had partaken most sparingly of wine'. But Wolfe was almost a teetotaller and on this occasion may well have been a good deal more drunk than Temple realized. Drunk or not, he was that evening, Temple decided, very rude and very odd. It must be said, however, that Temple enjoyed telling a story and no doubt made the most of this one.

Certainly Wolfe was in a mood of great excitement. At last, after all the petty difficulties and delays, the fleet was ready to put to sea. The stores and the few troops that were to sail with him were assembled at Spithead. It was his last night in London, a place he was always pleased to leave, for he disliked it and always felt ill and depressed when he had to stay there. The waiting was over. The next day he would depart for the coast and the dreaded sea voyage would soon begin.

Before leaving he wrote a letter to his mother. It was stiff and formal as usual and written in that carefully ordered style which constant practice had brought to a sort of gracefulness.

DEAR MADAM [it began, as always],
The formality of taking leave should be as much as possible

37

avoided; therefore I pray this method of offering my good wishes and duty to my father and to you. I shall carry this business through with my best abilities. The rest, you know, is in the hands of Providence, to whose care I hope your good life and conduct will recommend your son. Saunders talks of sailing on Thursday if the wind comes fair. . . . I heartily wish you health and happiness and easy enjoyment of the many good things which have fallen to your share.

My best duty to the General.

I am, dear Madam,

Your obedient and affectionate son,

JAM. WOLFE

London, Monday morn.

4

ONCE again Wolfe had to endure a rough and painfully slow crossing. The seas ran high, the winds
were adverse, and although the fleet had sailed
from Spithead on 14 February it was not until the end of
April that the creaking, laden ships tacked into Gabarus
Bay.

But the waters in Louisbourg Harbour were still not free
from ice, and Admiral Saunders had to lead his ships south-
ward down the coast of Nova Scotia, through clouds of
dense and swirling fog, to Halifax and a safe harbour.

At Halifax he found Admiral Durell with his small
flotilla which had left England some weeks before the main
fleet with orders to sail into the Gulf of St Lawrence as
soon as the ice melted and prevent any French reinforcements or provisions getting through to Quebec. Durell
told Saunders that he had not been able to get away before
owing to the sickness of his crews and the late season, and
was waiting for news that the ice in the Gulf had broken.
Fearful that he had already left it too late and that French
troop-ships and provision-boats would slip down the St
Lawrence River ahead of him, Wolfe offered the 'incompetent' Durell three hundred of his own men under
Colonel Carleton to supplement his crews and to occupy the
important islands in the St Lawrence channel. Saunders,
also annoyed by Durell's lack of spirit, ordered him to set
sail immediately with the three hundred men from the army.
But owing to unfavourable winds it was not until 5 May that
Durell was able to get out of Halifax Harbour. And by the
time he reached the St Lawrence a French convoy from

Boulogne had, as Wolfe feared, passed upstream ahead of him to take supplies and messages of warning and encouragement to Quebec.

Time was slipping past, and in these cold, northern waters time was precious.

A week went by in Halifax, and Wolfe bore it with impatience. The day he landed he had complained to both Amherst and Pitt about the shortage of men. 'I wish you health and success', he had added in his letter to Amherst. 'Of the former I have but a small share; of the latter as little hope, unless we get into the river first.' Half the troops in the Halifax garrison had measles, and it seemed unlikely that the army would number anything like the 12,000 men which had been promised him. He did not expect when he got to Louisbourg to have more than 9,000, and these would probably include about six companies of those 'dirtiest, most contemptible, cowardly dogs', the Americans. The British troops, however, he told Pitt in a strangely complimentary mood, were 'good and very well disposed. If valour can make amends for want of numbers, we shall probably succeed.'

At last on 13 May the men who had collected at Halifax were put aboard the boats, and the fleet sailed north for Louisbourg.

The scars of the siege in the year before were still everywhere visible in the bleak little stone and timber town. The masonry of the battlements had been patched, the mantlets and parapet walls rebuilt, and the breaches in the walls had been filled. But behind the walls many of the wooden houses were charred and empty, and in the middle of the town heaps of rubble lay in open spaces where once groups of buildings had stood.

On arrival at Louisbourg Wolfe was handed the orders which had been sent from London the year before and a bundle of letters. One of the letters was from his mother, and in it she told him of the death of his father several weeks before. The news did not come as a shock to him, for he had left the old General a sick man and he had not expected to see him again. But he had been fond of him, and his mother's sad letter distressed him. The next day he wore a thick black band around his sleeve and threw himself with so much energy into his work that even those who knew him well were surprised by his endless industry.

The troops were kept perpetually busy, practising their arms drill, cleaning their uniforms and muskets, learning new exercises, marching and countermarching through the streets of the town and beside the harbour walls. Almost every day a new order came from the General's headquarters, giving instructions about rations, about ammunition and medical inspections; limiting the supply of provisions for women; detailing the procedure to be observed by the troops when in transports, how a light infantryman should wear his equipment and where he should carry his tomahawk. Nothing was forgotten; no detail was too small to be considered.

In this bustle of constant activity the troops were able to overcome the depressing effects of the raw cold air and of the overcast sky from which the rain would suddenly pour down as if the clouds had burst. As abruptly as it had begun the rain would stop, and great waves of fog would come down, enveloping the garrison and harbour and the grey sea in damp, impenetrable white; while through the fog gusts of ice-cold wind would blow across the harbour walls from Labrador and the frozen expanses of the North Atlantic. In the harbour enormous floes of ice still floated round the ships, and through the mist the soldiers watched the sure-footed sailors in their dirty, ragged clothes leaping from floe to floe with boathooks in their hands, maintaining their balance with wonderful agility.

On 4 June the army was ready and the soldiers embarked. There were about 8,500 of them in the three brigades. In Monckton's brigade were five regiments of foot:

41

Amherst's 15th (later to become the East Yorkshire Regiment and now to be known as the Prince of Wales's Own Regiment of Yorkshire), Kennedy's 43rd (the Oxfordshire and Buckinghamshire Light Infantry, 1st Greenjackets), Anstruther's 58th (the 2nd Battalion of the Northamptonshire Regiment, the 2nd East Anglian Regiment), and Fraser's Highlanders—the 78th (disbanded in 1763). Under Townshend's command were Bragg's 28th (the Royal Gloucestershire Regiment), Lascelles' 47th (the Loyals) and the 2nd Battalion of the Royal Americans, the 60th (the King's Royal Rifle Corps, the 2nd Greenjackets); while Murray commanded Otway's 35th (the Royal Sussex Regiment), Webb's 48th (the 1st Battalion of the Northamptonshire Regiment, the 2nd East Anglian Regiment), and the 3rd Battalion of the Royal Americans. In addition to these ten regiments of the line were three companies of grenadiers from the Louisbourg garrison, three companies of light infantry,[1] and six companies of tough American rangers under Major Scott ('not complete', so Wolfe told his uncle, 'and the worst soldiers in the universe'). Each company of seventy-five men was allowed to take three women, and each company of a hundred men four women.[2]

It was a foggy, almost windless day, and the ships struggled with flapping sails to work their way out of the harbour. Only a few of them managed it, and the rest turned

[1] It had now become common practice in the Army for the light infantry and grenadier companies of the various infantry battalions to be taken away from their regiments and to be formed into battalions of their own. As the men chosen for these special duties had been the strongest and most alert in their original regiments, the light infantry and grenadier battalions were considered *élite* corps.

[2] This was a smaller proportion than was usually permitted. Regiments on active service were normally allowed at least six women for every hundred men. These soldiers' wives were not taken merely for the pleasure and companionship of the soldiers, but were expected to perform many duties in the field and, in particular, to act as nurses in the hospitals. Lots were drawn to decide which women should accompany the troops, but a commanding officer would often look the other way when the soldiers smuggled aboard the transports women who had drawn tickets reading 'Not to go'. Soldiers and their wives were not expected to take marriages very seriously. Some soldiers had as many as four or five wives in various towns or countries, and the widows would marry again within hours of their husbands being killed in action. Apart from the wives there were a number of female sutlers attached to the Army, and most of these acted as spare-time prostitutes. The sutlers did not travel with the regiments of the line, but in separate transports.

back to wait for a more favourable wind. The next day was as foggy as the day before, but the wind had freshened slightly so that most of the remaining ships were able to get out of the harbour. At midday, however, the wind blew up strongly from the north and the ships that had not cleared the land were forced back once more into the bay. Outside in the open sea the main fleet lay at anchor waiting for the few landlocked ships to join them. Although it was drizzling with rain, the air was milder and when the skies momentarily cleared the soldiers in the transports, their uniforms turned inside out to keep them clean, came up on deck to use the fishing lines and hooks with which a thoughtful commissariat had supplied them.

At four o'clock the following morning the last ship passed the lighthouse opposite the garrison and sailed out to join the fleet. Anchors were weighed as the signals were seen through the dark, early morning mist, and the convoy sailed away to the north. The wind was fresh now, and as dawn broke the mists were swept away and the skies were clear. At five o'clock that afternoon Newfoundland came into sight, covered still with snow, and then at last the sun came out and it was warm again.

For a week the seventeen sloops of war, the five frigates, and the crowded transports and store-ships sped quickly and steadily on, with full sails and flags streaming, through the Gulf of St Lawrence, past the pine-covered island of Anticosti towards the mouth of the great, wide St Lawrence River. And then on 16 June an officer suffering from scurvy on board one of the transports was advised by the surgeon to drink sea-water, instead of the ordinary ships' drinking-water, which was purified with ginger. When the bucket was hauled up over the side the water was found to be almost fresh. They were in the mouth of the river. The next day they saw land again.

For two hundred miles they sailed calmly upstream towards Quebec and the heart of Canada. Lining the river bank as far as the eye could stretch were dense, unbroken forests without sign of life or movement except when a flight of white-winged crossbills fluttered out across the water. In the shallows at the river's edge scores of walruses, white as snow, splashed and played and flicked their whiskers indifferently as the soldiers fired at them and the balls bounced off their backs; while schools of porpoises and seals, swimming and jumping across the wake of the ships, threw up showers of silvery spray from the dark water. The weather was still fine and warm and the spirits of the men were high. The officers drank a cheerful daily toast at the mess tables to 'British Colours on every French fort, post and garrison in America'.

Meanwhile farther upstream the officers in Durell's flotilla, including James Cook, then master of the *Pembroke*, were busy taking soundings in the perilous waters ahead and leaving markers and buoys for the guidance of the main fleet.

On the fifteenth day of the voyage the weather broke, and the calm of the voyage was momentarily shattered by a violent storm which lashed the river into fury as the wind howled down from the mountains and the rain poured on to the battened decks. When the storm died away and the wind dropped, the convoy was almost becalmed as it struggled towards Tadoussac, where the fast-flowing Saguennay River, swollen by the melting snows and ice of Lake St John, cascaded into the main stream. The ships, without wind in their sails to get them quickly past the swirling cross-currents, were borne along helplessly in the turbulent waters, astonishingly saved from collision by the agile sailors, who jumped about the decks laughing at the soldiers' concern.

All the ships got through without mishap, but the pleasures of the voyage were over. Now the dense forests along the river bank were broken here and there by the clearings of Canadian settlements, and at night on the high ground could be seen the fiercely burning beacons

44

warning the French outposts of the invading fleet's approach. Sometimes a settler, hidden behind a log at the water's edge, would take a shot at the sailors in the sounding boats which sailed nearer to the bank than the other ships to mark the edge of the narrowing channel. For wide as the river still was, the dangers of running aground on a submerged reef of rock or mud were now very real, and the navigable channel was with every mile growing more difficult to discern.

At Ile aux Coudres, where the fleet anchored on 24 June, Admiral Saunders decided that local knowledge must be sought before he risked his ships in the even more treacherous waters between there and the Basin of Quebec. Fortunately, it was at Ile aux Coudres that he had arranged to meet Admiral Durell's squadron ; and Durell was able to supply him with several Canadian pilots. Captain Knox of Kennedy's Regiment learned from a midshipman in Durell's squadron how the Admiral had come by these pilots. It appeared that on approaching Ile aux Coudres he had hoisted the white flag of the French Navy and that within half an hour several boats had pulled out from the river banks bringing pilots towards the various ships of the British squadron. As each pilot stepped on board his chosen ship he was arrested as a prisoner-of-war and told that if he refused to pilot the ship through the shallows, or if it went aground, he would be hanged from the mainmast.

At three o'clock in the afternoon of 25 June one of these impressed pilots came aboard Captain Knox's transport, the *Goodwill*, protesting vigorously at the dishonest trick played upon him and his companions and shouting in voluble French that Canada would be the grave of the whole British army and that the walls of Quebec would soon be ornamented with English scalps. Captain Killick, the old master of the *Goodwill*, having a sailor's traditional contempt for Gallic excitement, pushed the furious Canadian out of the way and said that he'd have no damned Frog piloting his ship. He told his mate to take the helm and he went himself to the fo'c'sle with his speaking-trumpet. The colonel in charge of the troops on board shouted at him not to be such a fool, as he would surely drive the ship aground or rip its bottom out. 'Aye, aye, me dear,' Killick said, wagging his finger at the colonel. 'But damme if I don't convince you an Englishman shall go where a Frenchman dares not show his nose.' And he stumped off to the bow of his ship.

The colonel called to the ship behind them in the narrow deep-water channel to watch out as the *Goodwill* was without a pilot. 'Who's your master?' yelled the captain of the following ship. 'It's old Killick', shouted Killick himself through his trumpet, 'and that's enough.' And it seemed indeed that it was. Leaning over the bow, chatting and joking imperturbably with the sailors in the sounding boats below, giving orders to the helmsman with profound unconcern, he guided the *Goodwill* through the twisting· channel. Captain Knox went forward to watch him, and Killick pointed out to him the different shades of blue and grey indicating the likely depth, the scarcely discernible but telltale ripples disturbing the surface of the water, the waves now running smoothly, now halting and dropping away from a submerged ridge. Occasionally the men in the sounding boats would shout a warning or point out the places where they thought the water was shallow. 'Aye, aye, me dears,' Killick told them reassuringly, having seen the danger before them, missing nothing. 'Aye, aye. Chalk it down.'

As the *Goodwill* came out of the zigzag channel and into the clearer water, the old master put down his trumpet and handed over the ship to his mate. 'Well, damme,' he said to him. 'Damme if there are not a thousand places in the Thames more hazardous than this; I am ashamed that Englishmen should make such a rout about it.'

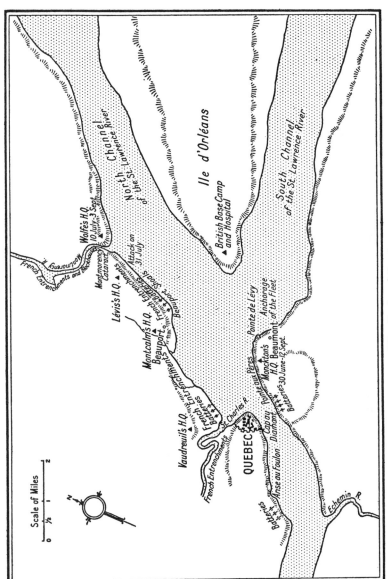

The Basin of Quebec

Following the *Goodwill*, the other transports came through safely, one after the other, the coloured flags in the sounding boats fluttering gaily in the breeze, and by the evening of 26 June the whole fleet, with many more war-ships than Wolfe had expected to come up so far, was anchored off Ile d'Orléans, a big island more than twenty miles long and five miles wide which lay in the middle of the St Lawrence River opposite the Basin of Quebec.

From here it was possible to see something of the im-pressive grandeur and strength of the enemy's position. The sight was awe-inspiring to the least imaginative soldier. Across the Basin of Quebec, high above the river on its rocky cliff, like a medieval fortress, stood the town itself, its thick and solid walls flying the French flag from each corner and seeming defiantly to invite assault.

To the left and right of the town, stretching out of sight in each direction, the steep brown cliffs rose sheer from the shallows to the French entrenchments lining the summit. Scarred here and there by a deep ravine, their face was barren and lifeless. Loose rocks and slipping shale made climbing up them perilous, and from many points im-possible. The few dry shrubs, the stunted spruce and cedar and blasted-looking black hawthorn and choke-cherry, emphasized the quiet deadness of these forbidding slopes, which, far away to the right, were broken open by the torrent of the cataract that pours the plunging waters of the Montmorency River into the St Lawrence, two hundred and fifty feet below it.

Seen in that clear, late evening light, it was a magnificent if foreboding landscape, but it was also, as Wolfe was later despairingly to tell Pitt, from a soldier's point of view, 'the strongest country in the world'.

5

THE Governor of Canada, the Marquis de Vaudreuil, was horrified. So sure had he been that the river was not navigable by ships of any size that he had not thought it worth while to place cannon on the heights of Tourmente from where they might have blasted the British fleet out of the river during their slow progress through the channel. 'The enemy', he wrote to the Minister of Marine and Colonies in Paris, 'has passed sixty ships of war where we hardly dared risk a vessel of a hundred tons.' He did not for one moment consider, however, that this would make any difference to the outcome of the forthcoming siege. As he had already informed the Minister in letters of outrageous self-laudation, he had taken steps to ensure that Quebec was impregnable.

The enthusiasm with which I am fired for the service of the King [he assured him] will always enable me to overcome the greatest obstacles. I am taking every possible measure to give the enemy a good reception whenever he may attack us. . . . There is no trick, no expedience, no means which my zeal does not suggest to set traps for them and when necessary to fight them with a fervour, and indeed a fury, which exceeds the scope of their ambitious plans. . . . My enthusiasm is generally applauded. It has penetrated every heart; all men say aloud: 'We shall die in the ruins of Canada, our native land, before we surrender to the English.'

His bravely voiced confidence in the determined spirit of the defenders of Quebec seemed, however, to some of his subordinates hardly justified. The French regular troops were, they knew, sound enough; but there were only five

49

regiments of them. And no more could be expected. Colonel de Bougainville, who had been sent to France the year before with a request for reinforcements, had just returned to Quebec, slipping past Admiral Durell's squadron in a thick fog, with scarcely more than three hundred men who were all that could be spared from the army in Europe. The main strength of the admittedly large defending force was comprised of colony troops and Canadian militiamen, who, called up suddenly from their farms and settlements, ambled into Quebec, angry and sullen at being once more asked to fight the English, from whom, they protested, the home country ought by rights to defend them ; while their Indian allies, ferocious and terrifying as they were in attack, had neither the inclination nor the temperament patiently to withstand a siege. Even their large numbers were in one way a disadvantage, for food was short and the militiamen were annoyed at being given the same meagre ration of two ounces of bread a day as the civilians in the town. This ration might have been more had it not been for the flagrant inefficiency and corruption of the authorities in general and of Bigot, the Intendant, in particular. Bigot, whose full title of *Intendant de Justice, Police et Finance* gives some idea of the scope of his powers and influence, had for years been cheating his Government and lining his pockets at the expense of the Canadian people and even now in a time of crisis continued to do so. Bigot had been appointed Intendant in 1748 and had immediately made a profitable arrangement with a business concern in Bordeaux through which he purchased supplies for Canada. His frauds and extortions made him an enormous fortune. For a minor outbreak of smallpox in an Indian tribe he had once debited the Treasury with a million francs ; when soil was needed for the fortifications of Quebec, where there was little earth above the hard rock, he had paid the contractors by the load—and a load was no more than a handful. He encouraged his assistants to follow his example. Joseph

Cadet, who was the son of a Quebec butcher, began his career as clerk in the Intendant's office and finished it as the extremely wealthy Baron de la Touche Avrigny. 'Profit by your place, my dear Vergor', Bigot wrote to another of his fellow-parasites. 'You are free to do as you like.'

The Governor, himself, was not known to be connected with these frauds but gave their perpetrators his unquestioning support. He was a Canadian, the son of a former Governor of Canada, and he resented the interference of Frenchmen who did not understand the country. When the Commander-in-Chief, the Marquis de Montcalm, wrote to Paris with specific charges against the Canadian civil administration, Vaudreuil replied that Bigot had his full confidence. 'Nobody is a better citizen than he', he said, 'or has the King's interest more at heart.'

Vaudreuil may even have believed this. Although never accused of dishonesty, he was vain, incompetent, and dull and found it difficult to recognize dishonesty in others, particularly in those who flattered him. Montcalm thought him somewhat stupid. He had done his best to get on with him and at first he had been successful. 'I am on good terms with him', he wrote to the Minister of War, 'but not in his confidence, which he never gives to anybody from France. His intentions are good, but he is slow and irresolute.'

The wary pretence of friendship did not last. Montcalm was an interloper in the Governor's opinion. But he was also more than that. He was a man of distinguished birth and unassailable reputation. Vaudreuil, despite his conceit, was jealous of the urbane, sardonic, handsome Frenchman and often reminded him of the Canadian Governor's ultimate authority in all things. The Commander-in-Chief was authorized only 'to give orders provisionally'.

It was a situation which a less affable man would have found intolerable. But Montcalm accepted it, if not uncomplainingly, at least with a cynical good-humour. He hoped that when the time came for action Vaudreuil would have enough sense to leave it to him to decide what to do. In the meantime, although he did not care for Canada or the Canadians and longed to return to his estate in the south of France and to his family, he made the most of the gaiety of Quebec, the balls and parties, the receptions and dinners. He did not share Bigot's passion for gambling, but he did appreciate the charms of Bigot's mistress.

Vaudreuil had less capacity for enjoying himself and distrusted Frenchmen who had. He called councils of war almost daily. At these meetings colonial officials, Indian chiefs, and Army and militia officers gave their opinions vociferously and without attention to the views of anyone else. They shouted and quarrelled, waving their arms in the air like English caricatures of Frenchmen, until Montcalm was obliged to ask each of them in turn to put his views into writing so that they might be considered in circumstances more conducive to concentration.

Montcalm himself was occasionally to be seen as excited and irritated as any of them, for although normally an even-tempered man he was neither placid nor patient; and his dislike of the more uncouth of the Canadian officers was obvious.

But in spite of these fruitless and agitated meetings, in spite of Vaudreuil's jealousy of Montcalm and Montcalm's growing contempt for Vaudreuil, by the time the pennants on the masts of the British fleet could be seen from the ramparts of Quebec the French defences were complete.

Montcalm, after many consultations with his able second-in-command de Lévis and his aide-de-camp de Bougainville, and after listening to the hundreds of suggestions put forward at Vaudreuil's incoherent councils of war, had eventually decided to concentrate his main force to the east of the town along the steep cliffs overlooking the St Lawrence River. It was a position of exceptional natural strength, as Wolfe had seen. For six miles between the St Charles

River on his right and the cataract of Montmorency on his left, his well-sited entrenchments commanded the river. From his headquarters in the village of Beauport at the centre of the line he could keep in touch with Lévis who commanded the troops along the Montmorency River and with Governor Ramezay who commanded the garrison in Quebec itself. And beyond Quebec several strong detachments guarded every place where troops might land and attempt to scale the cliffs between the town and Cap Rouge seven miles upstream towards Montreal.

The high, commanding position of each entrenchment and its wide field of fire across the river so far below gave the defenders every confidence. If the English tried to attack them, an officer in the Regiment of La Sarre wrote, they would be able to pick them off like sitting ducks in the boats, and if any of them did manage to reach the bottom of the cliff and to clamber up the steep and slippery slope, they would be met by a hail of ball and shot which would roll them back into the river. Bougainville had already said that he thought Quebec could be defended by three or four thousand men against all-comers and although he did not believe the English would 'make any attempt against it, they might nevertheless have the madness to do so' and it was as well to be prepared against surprise.

The French were certainly well prepared. They had more than four times as many men as Bougainville thought necessary; they had well over a hundred cannon mounted in positions which Montcalm had had time carefully to select, and several floating batteries and gun-boats anchored in the river. They were, moreover, occupying a natural line of defence on chosen ground in their own country. Their fortifications were well constructed and they outnumbered the enemy almost two to one.

'Quebec', Vaudreuil assured Versailles, with understandable confidence, 'is impregnable.'

6

LATE at night on 26 June, about six hours after the fleet had anchored off Ile d'Orléans, Lieutenant Meech, a young officer from Connecticut, landed on the island with forty American rangers. They crept slowly up the wooded slopes of the southern shore, muskets in hand, knives and tomahawks hanging from their belts. It was a dark night and they could scarcely see the trunks of the trees as they advanced inland. The wind had dropped and the leaves stood still in the silence. It seemed that the island was deserted. They came to a log cabin in a clearing, but it was empty and there were no animals in the compound. And then, just beyond the compound, they heard voices and crawled slowly forward towards them. Through the undergrowth they saw a group of men, the light from an oil lamp reflected on their faces, lowering a chest into a hole in the ground. Without orders from Lieutenant Meech the rangers jumped to their feet and opened fire. The Canadian settlers grabbed their guns and returned the fire before running off into the woods. Most of the shots whined harmlessly between the trees, but one of them at least found its mark and a ranger fell dead, shot through the chest. His companions reloaded and ran after the fleeing Canadians, shouting and cursing as they stumbled through the thick undergrowth, letting off an occasional shot blindly into the darkness.

But the settlers got clean away and when Lieutenant Meech ordered his men to halt, the deep, unnerving silence came down once more between the trees. Thinking that the settlers might perhaps be lying in wait for them somewhere in the darkness ahead, and afraid that by advancing he might take his men into an ambush, Meech led them back to the farmhouse so that they might spend the few remaining hours of darkness there before patrolling the rest of the island.

At dawn they came out again and in the dim light they found the body of the man who had been shot the night before. His flesh had been slashed to the bone in several places, his hands almost severed from the wrists, and he had been neatly scalped. His body had been nailed to the ground by a stake driven through his stomach. The sight of the butchered corpse made little impression on the hardened rangers, who had lived for years accepting the fact that they too might end their lives mangled and scalpless like this. And being inured to butchery, many of them had become butchers themselves. Violence had bred violence, and rangers scalped Indians with as little compunction as the Indians scalped them.

Whether the ranger had been scalped by Indians or Canadians his companions could not tell, for when that morning they continued their patrol across the island, through the woods and the well-cultivated fields, to the eastern shore, they found that it had been deserted and they were able to return unmolested to the boats and to report that so far as they could discover all the inhabitants had gone.

Within a few hours the entire army had disembarked and were drawn up in battle formation on the beach. The garrison in Quebec, looking across the river in the clear morning light, could see quite plainly the rows and squares and half-circles of red and white. Down by the shore they watched the lines of artillerymen dragging the cannon up the beach, the stores being unloaded, the group of sutlers busily moving round the softly smoking fires, the staff officers talking in the yard of the church of St Lawrence.

Fixed to the door of this church Captain Knox was

amused to find a notice written in excessively polite terms by the parish priest. The priest respectfully hoped that the English officers would see that no harm came to his church or to his house next door to it. He regretted that they had not come earlier, as then they might have enjoyed the delicious radishes and asparagus in his garden, which were now unhappily going to seed.

When the last soldier had got ashore and the last ammunition box had been unloaded, the army was marched about a mile to the north-east and was encamped facing the river in a single line; while General Wolfe with Major Mackellar, the Chief Engineer, and his two aides-de-camp went with an escort of light infantry to reconnoitre the island and to take a first survey of the enemy's position.

From a high point about two miles east of the army, where the ground fell sharply away to the river, Wolfe looked through his telescope at Quebec and realized for the first time the true magnitude of the task which Pitt had set him. Opposite him, either side of the church and the little village of Beauport, he could see the rows of white tents along the summit of the high cliffs, the feather-topped wigwams, the irregular banks of loose, stony earth in front of the entrenchments, the stone white-washed houses and the wooden cabins with their windows reduced to slits by the logs piled inside the frames. The town of Quebec he saw as Mackellar had described it in his report, the Upper Town white and beautiful in the sunlight, the straggling buildings of the Lower Town disappearing out of sight behind Cap au Diamant. The Lower Town with its wharves, warehouses, and cottages, although protected (Mackellar estimated) by twenty-four guns, looked as if it might be easy enough to take, but any force which occupied it would then be bombarded from the unassailable heights above.

Beyond the town, upsteam towards Montreal, the high and rugged banks continued as far as Cap Rouge seven miles to the west. Wolfe slowly turned his telescope back again along the arc of the steep brown cliffs, from the precipitous declivities beyond Quebec, past the town to the thundering waterfall at Montmorency so safely guarding the French flank. Mackellar and his aides-de-camp watched him as he stood there, his tall, thin body quite still and only his head moving slowly from side to side as he brought his telescope round. He held the glass delicately, a soldier noticed, clasping the brass eye-piece with long, thin hands the backs of which were disfigured by the marks left by a recent attack of scurvy. He stopped for minutes at a time to study a ravine or a possible landing-place and then moved the glass on again, making no comment, nodding sometimes as Mackellar spoke to him but otherwise tense and silent. And then with a gesture of impatient petulance he snapped the telescope together and marched back to camp.

Wolfe had seen enough to realize that his original plan of attack, made at Louisbourg after a careful study of Mackellar's maps and sketches, would have to be abandoned. It had been based on the assumption that the French would concentrate their forces in and around Quebec itself and that he would consequently be able to land most of his troops somewhere between the St Charles and Montmorency rivers and then advance quickly behind the town and throw up siege works on the plains to the west of it. But the obviously strong entrenchments all along the cliffs, commanding every possible landing-place, made such an enterprise extremely hazardous. It was going to be much more difficult than he had expected. He would have to think again.

On his way back to camp he was irritated by the numbers of soldiers he saw on the pilfering forays which English soldiers so much enjoy. Out of the woods they came, driving pigs and goats, carrying hens and vegetables, with armfuls of wood for their fires and straw for their tents, shouting at each other excitedly, some of them a little drunk. He was already in a dispirited mood after the sight of the formidable

57

position which the enemy was occupying, and his depression was increased by this display of unmilitary mudlarking which the officers were apparently doing nothing to prevent. As soon as he got back to his billet he drafted a General Order which reflected his irritation. The following day the order was posted up at the headquarters of all companies. 'Whenever the Regiments send for straw *or anything else they want*', the order ran, 'proper officers must go with their men to prevent such irregularities as the General saw yesterday, and will be obliged to punish very severely.'

It was a sad, discouraging day and sudden cold gusts of wind blew across the river and whined between the trees. In the distance the sky was black and the air was full of an oppressive expectancy and the faint, electric crackle of lightning. The storm awaited all day with gloomy impatience broke violently in the late afternoon, and the heavy rain poured down as the thunder roared and the wind raced down the river dashing the ships together at their moorings. Several of the smaller boats were thrown ashore by the surging water and were shattered on the rocks, and many of the flat-bottomed landing-craft overturned and sank or were broken to pieces as they fell and smashed together in the deep and suddenly forming troughs.

As night fell the storm abated and the soldiers in the forward sentry posts bailed the water out of their entrenchments in the pitch blackness and surreptitiously got out their secret stores of rum.

At eleven o'clock one of them on duty at Pointe d'Orléans told his companion that he thought he could see something in the river floating downstream towards them. For a few seconds they stared ahead into the darkness and then, quite distinctly, they saw flashes of light and the glow of torches and heard the sound of excited voices. A few moments later the darkness was blown away in a sudden brilliant explosion and a cascade of flames and sparks. Sheets of fire leapt out of the river in a series of deafening roars, while pieces of burning wood shot high into the air and showers of metal flew above the sentries' heads and tore with a rush of air into the trees behind them. Frightened out of their wits by the infernal uproar, the sentries jumped out of their trenches and ran back in panic towards the main lines, some shouting that the enemy had a terrible secret weapon, others that it was an earthquake. As they ran the explosions behind them grew louder and louder and billows of suffocating smoke poured across the river and filled the air with the smell of sulphur.

Out of range of the flying metal the troops farther inland could watch the display with more excitement than fear. For the shapes in the river were now clearly recognizable in the light of the flames as nothing more unnatural or infernal than fireships, explosively drifting towards the island and the British ships at anchor off its western shore. As they floated across, flames shot along the tar-soaked troughs cut in their decks and leapt up the masts and over the rigging, which was coated with melted resin ; barrels of pitch and boxes of grenades exploded beneath the battened decks and blew the jagged iron covers off the port-holes ; while old muskets and spiked cannon, sprinkled with powder and with quantities of ball and shot rammed down their barrels, burst open and sent volleys of red-hot metal and gushes of sparks in every direction. 'They were certainly', Captain Knox thought, 'the grandest fireworks (if I may be allowed to call them so) that can possibly be conceived.'

Had the French crews waited longer before setting light to the trains of tar and powder, the British officers could not have watched the oncoming ships with such calm and fascinated pleasure. But as it was, the sailors on watch on the ships at anchor had several minutes' warning of their approach and were able to row out with cables and grappling-hooks to intercept the fireships before any damage was done. As some of the hulks ran aground, still burning fiercely and sulkily belching out clouds of smoke and occasional volleys of grapeshot, the sailors threw their grappling-hooks aboard the others and towed them downstream to beach them at a safe distance from their own ships, as skilfully and confidently as if they had spent their lives practising the manœuvre.

By now the riverside was as light as if it were day. The grounded hulks and those being towed away burned so brightly that the British troops, drawn up in battle formation lest the French should attack, could see quite clearly the lines of tents on the cliffs opposite them.

Behind his soldiers, from the steeple of the little church of Beauport, Vaudreuil watched the scene with growing disappointment and anger. The fireships had cost nearly two million francs, and the waste of money depressed him. He was also furious with the crews for firing the ships and jumping clear so soon, and dismayed to hear that the one captain and his crew of seven men who had bravely waited until their ship was dangerously near the British fleet had been trapped and burned alive.

But although the fireships had failed in their main intended purpose, they had succeeded in throwing the outposts into momentary confusion ; and this, if he had known it, would have encouraged him. Certainly it infuriated Wolfe, who ordered the officer in charge of them to be arrested. The arrest of this conscientious and popular officer was an action which he immediately regretted. Several of the young man's friends made application on his behalf for his release and the kind-hearted Brigadier Monckton added his recommendation to theirs, emphasizing his excellent character and previously admirable service. When Wolfe gave in and ordered his release, at least one young officer thought that he could not in all fairness have done otherwise. For surely the General should have seen that his men were told what to expect? Mackellar, the Chief Engineer, had informed him before he left England that the French had many fireships at Quebec ; but the sentries were not warned and when they saw the dark, mysterious shapes in the river suddenly spit into raging life, they lost their nerve and fled, and, suspicious and ignorant as they were, he did not find it surprising that they had done so.

The officer was not alone in his implied rebuke. And so the incident of the unsuccessful fireships was important in at least this one respect. There was a feeling, as yet unexpressed, that a mistake had been made. The General felt the first cold breath of reproach.

7

WEST of Ile d'Orléans, across the south channel
of the St Lawrence River, a high elbow of land
juts out towards Quebec. Along the southerly
curve of this elbow the St Lawrence is less than a mile wide
and the opposite banks are within cannon shot of each other.
If it were possible to occupy this part of the shore, the
admirals suggested, British batteries on the cliffs could cover
the passage of ships into the upper river and thus threaten
the French line of supply between the town and Montreal.
A British occupation of the heights here would also make
it possible for the fleet to use a safer anchorage than at
present it enjoyed.

Montcalm, realizing the possible danger of this, had
suggested that Pointe de Lévy, as the elbow was called,
should be held by a well-entrenched force of four thousand
men; but his suggestion had been rejected. Vaudreuil
agreed that an English battery might give the Lower Town
a bad time, but their cannon would certainly not have the
elevation to reach the Upper Town, which could return
their fire with devastating effect and blow the British guns
into the river. He doubted that the British would, in any
case, be able to gain a footing on the point and dig in a
battery under the heavy fire which it would be possible to
rain down upon them not only from Quebec but also from
floating batteries on the river. Pointe de Lévy was, therefore, left to a small force of Canadians and Indians whose
orders were to hold off any invading troops until the
French batteries were able to blast them back across the
south channel.

On the afternoon of 29 June, with the fireships still smouldering behind them, a small force of light infantry and American rangers from Monckton's brigade crossed the channel and clambered up the steep, unguarded banks of Pointe de Lévy towards the group of buildings round the small white church of Beaumont. It was a cold afternoon with a strong north wind and the ground underfoot was still hard with frost as the Americans and light infantrymen cautiously approached the apparently unoccupied hamlet.

It was alarmingly quiet. Even the batteries across the river were silent. The men walked into Beaumont and pushed open the doors of the few buildings, suspecting a trap. But they were all empty. They went into the church and that too was empty. And then as a group of rangers advanced along the path beyond the church, the strange silence was broken by a rattle of shots.

Relieved by this sudden return to predictable events and a known enemy, the rangers enthusiastically took cover and within a few minutes had crawled round to a position behind the inexperienced Canadians. In the short fight that followed they killed seven of them and took five prisoner. As the rest escaped into the woods the five prisoners watched as their seven dead comrades were scalped with matter-of-fact efficiency by the Americans.

The prisoners were sent back to Ile d'Orléans with a message that the objective had been successfully occupied.

At seven o'clock the next morning Monckton crossed to Pointe de Lévy with the rest of his brigade and joined the patrol of light infantry and rangers in Beaumont. He carried with him a proclamation signed by Wolfe, which he fixed to the church door.

Britain [the proclamation announced in pedantic French to the abandoned village] stretches out a powerful yet merciful hand. . . . The King of Great Britain does not wage war against the Industrious Peasant, the sacred order of Religion, or defenceless

Women or Children. . . . The people may remain unmolested. . . .
But if by a vain obstinacy and misguided valour they presume to
appear in arms, they must expect the most Fatal Consequences;
their habitations destroyed, their sacred temples exposed to an
exasperated soldiery, their harvest utterly ruined. . . . The miserable
Canadians must in the winter have the mortification of seeing the
very families, for whom they have been exerting but a fruitless
and indiscreet bravery, perish by the most dismal Want and Famine.

Leaving this notice to be torn down next day by a disdainful Canadian villager, Monckton went on with this
brigade along the riverside road towards the high ground
facing Quebec, leaving a small detachment of the 43rd
Regiment in the village. An hour and a half later an officer
with a sergeant and twelve men returned with orders for
the rearguard to follow the main body. At the same time
over the hill appeared 'six straggling fellows', their sepia
skins naked but for their loin-cloths and the blankets over
their shoulders. These Indians stood looking contemplatively down on the rear-guard for two or three minutes and
then beckoned to the soldiers to advance. The soldiers
declined the invitation and beckoned to the Indians. The
Indians raised their muskets and, with remarkable in-
accuracy, fired them. Continuing the curious, scorpion-like
ceremony, an officer of the rearguard advanced towards the
Indians with a white handkerchief tied to a bayonet
inviting them to surrender. And the Indians, growing tired
of the rather boring encounter, sauntered off, leaving the
rearguard free to advance, and at five o'clock they joined
Monckton, who had come up against strong resistance from
about six hundred Canadian troops supported by some
three hundred settlers and fifty Indians.

Monckton lost nearly thirty men driving the ill-trained
enemy from their strong positions on the heights overlooking
the Basin of Quebec, and it took him until nightfall to do so.
But it was not until the next day, and then long after dawn,
that the French sent out a floating battery in an effort to

dislodge him, and even then the batteries at Quebec remained silent. The floating battery, however, lobbing shells on to the cliff top, caused many casualties amongst the exposed and unprotected British troops, and a French ship sailing out from Quebec joined in the cannonading until the frigate *Trent* sailed upstream with all her guns blazing and forced her to sheer off. By then many of the red-coated soldiers lying face down on the rocky earth were dead or wounded, and there was a smell of powder and blood in the air. The war had begun.

All day long the soldiers hacked and scraped at the hard earth in their efforts to get below the surface before the expected bombardment began. But during that first day on the point the danger came not from the French cannons but from the Indians constantly rushing out at the soldiers on the flanks, firing wildly and brandishing their scalping-knives.

At three o'clock in the afternoon a larger band of Indians came yelling out of the scrub, some of them with their faces painted livid white, with blue and red stripes across their foreheads and down their cheeks, others wearing the furs and masks of animals. They dashed towards a section of soldiers, who threw down their tools to grab their muskets stacked beside the heaps of earth. But this time it was not only the British soldiers that the Indians had to fight, for lying in wait for them behind a fold in the cliff-top was a group of rangers.

The rangers waited until the Indians were well within their ambush before they opened fire. Nine Indians fell and the rest ran back to the woods, while the rangers added the dripping scalps of the fallen to their growing collection.

After this the Indians were not so confidently reckless in their raids and more dangerous. They crept up, mainly at night, towards the sentries on the outskirts of the British position and striking quickly and silently they crawled back again into the scrub, leaving the scalpless bodies of their victims to be found with a shiver of horror by the men who came to relieve them. Already several unwary outposts on Ile d'Orléans had been attacked in this swift and noiseless way, and the General Headquarters, angered by such unmilitary and ungentlemanly attacks, had issued orders stressing the necessity for extreme vigilance against these cowardly assaults from 'rascals who dare not show themselves'. It was ordered 'once and for all' on 28 June that 'soldiers are to keep close to their encampments, are not to pass without the out guards or wander through the country in the disorderly manner which has been observed here. . . . No sentrys are ever to be planted within point blank of musquet shot of a wood, unless behind stones or trees, so as not to be seen in a woody country. Detachments must *never* halt or encamp in the little openings in the woods, nor *ever* pass through them without examining them.'

But the attacks of the marauding Indians were among the least of Monckton's worries on Pointe de Lévy. Throughout 1 July he hourly expected a French counter-attack and the full force of the French batteries to open up on his exposed position before the soldiers had had time to dig themselves in below the level of the hard and stony earth, and before he could get his own guns dragged up the cliffs from the landing-place.

Progress in the British positions seemed painfully slow. The soldiers hacking at the rocky ground and tugging at the wheels of the cannon on the dangerous slopes worked all day long and through half the following night. Down by the river bank, working against time, helped by sailors and marines, they struggled under intermittent fire from the floating guns out in the basin, to erect a barbette battery before the French attacked. It was a cold, still night with the stars clear and bright in the sky, and the noise of the entrenching tools striking into the rocky ground could be heard loud and sharp in the darkness. The sentries on the cliff-top peered down towards the St Lawrence and over towards Quebec, but they saw nothing and heard only the clanking of the spades and bayonets behind them and the rumble of swearing voices. Just before dawn the order came to stand to, and the troops formed up, tired and ill-tempered, along the curve of the point facing Quebec. But the expected attack never came. The French position remained quiet and lifeless as though abandoned, and the British began their work once more in the growing light.

Fortunately for Monckton the French were in doubt as to the British intentions. During the afternoon of the previous day an English soldier had been captured and had immediately been taken across the river to Quebec. He assured Vaudreuil, either with a commendable intention to deceive or in real ignorance of what was intended, that the occupation of Pointe de Lévy was a feint and that a full-scale attack on the northern cliffs below the town would be made that night or the following one.

Vaudreuil had believed him, and the regiments between Quebec and the Montmorency cataract were alerted and reinforced. Montcalm at first approved the Governor's action, but when it became obvious that the enemy activities on Pointe de Lévy were more than a feint he changed his mind and sent Vaudreuil a letter strongly recommending an attack on the English positions before it was too late. Vaudreuil did not trouble to acknowledge the letter and ignored the advice it contained.

Early on the morning of 2 July Wolfe himself came over from Ile d'Orléans to select a place from which Quebec might be most effectively bombarded. He found a site at Pointe aux Pères about a mile west of Monckton's headquarters and digging began there within the hour. From Pointe aux Pères Wolfe could get a better view of Quebec than he had had before and saw closely for the first time the strong French entrenchments behind the town and the steep brown cliffs which fell down to the river as sharply here as by the Montmorency River. Around the town and amongst the warehouses and wooden shacks along the wharf he could see through his glass the numerous soldiers moving about like flies. But for every five coloured Canadian coats he saw, there was only one French uniform. It was a comfort of a sort, for so far he had seen no reason to change his profoundly contemptuous opinion of the fighting qualities of the Canadian militia and of the Canadian character in general.

It was a judgment which later on in the campaign he was given good cause to modify. And even as he watched Quebec, its inhabitants were planning with courage and excited confidence an attack upon the British position. Against his better judgment Montcalm had been persuaded to allow a mixed force of fifteen hundred Canadians to attempt the assault. Volunteers came forward from all over Quebec to join the motley rag-bag of a commando. Fishermen from the Lower Town and pupils from the seminary joined the Canadian troops from the garrison and Canadian settlers from the camps outside the town walls. A hundred and fifty French regulars volunteered to give the force a sprinkling of discipline, and several Indians covered with paint and smelling of brandy added a welcome look of ferocity. The whole ragged collection was put under the command of Captain Dumas, a brave officer in the Languedoc Regiment, who was experienced in guerrilla warfare. As soon as it was dark Dumas led them upstream to Sillery, four miles from Quebec, where they crossed the river unobserved, in spite of the noise they made in the boats and at the landing-places.

By now the excitement and enthusiasm had given way to a nervous anxiety. As they stumbled along the cliff-top towards the British position the amateur soldiers grew increasingly frightened. It had been easy enough to volunteer for a dangerous mission amidst the encouragement of friends and the admiration of women, the tearful pleadings of a family; but out here in the cold night, lonely and afraid in the darkness, it was difficult to maintain that former bravura. One of the seminary pupils, his finger on the trigger of his strange musket, saw, or thought he saw, in the night ahead, an English soldier ; and without waiting for an order he pulled the trigger in sudden panic.

The sharp crack of the musket shot broke the fading hope of success. The untrained Canadians, taut and dry-mouthed, lost their nerve. Two of the other students fired at their own patrol and then ran helter-skelter back towards their canoes. The rest of them, infected by the atmosphere of panic and alarmed by the noise of the British troops whose shouts of warning they took for war cries, immediately joined in the scramble to regain the boats, and nothing Dumas or the regulars could do prevented them. They rushed along the cliff-top, shouting and firing recklessly at each other, and stumbled down towards the landing-place. By six o'clock in the morning they were back at Quebec, exhausted and ashamed. But seventy of their comrades were left behind, dead or wounded on the river banks.

The French batteries had by now at last opened up, and for the next few days the British troops laboured to get their own batteries erected under a storm of shot and shell. Night and day as the shells fell unceasingly around them the soldiers and sailors struggled to get the gun emplacements ready so that they might reply to the constant cannonade. During these early days of July it was not only the French guns which made life unpleasant for Monckton's men, for the weather was appalling. On 3 July and again on 4 July the dark sky was often and abruptly lit by terrifying flashes of lightning, leaping and crackling out of the dark grey clouds, while the rain poured down through the wind and the thunder rolled and boomed over the water-filled trenches and the sodden, flapping tents. The morale of the men, bored and inactive on Ile d'Orléans and bombarded ceaselessly on Pointe de Lévy, fell lower and lower. And Wolfe tried to throw off his own reactive depression in constant activity.

Every day he crossed to Pointe de Lévy from his head-quarters on the island to see how the work on the batteries was progressing, and every night he spent long hours looking at his maps and sketches, wondering how best the enemy could be attacked.

The island seemed to be swarming with women. Each morning when the General went on his rounds he was irritated by the sight of the numerous dirty, untidy sutlers in their clumsy calico skirts and woollen bonnets, and by the even more distasteful spectacle of their petticoats and leather stays hanging between the trees. 'All orders relating to women', he wrote in a General Order which reflected his annoyance, 'must be read to them by the sergeants of their respective companies, so that they may not plead ignorance.' Only those women with specific authority to sutle in the camp were to be allowed to do so; the rest must be prevented immediately. Women refusing to serve as nurses in the field hospitals were to be struck off the provision roll. Camp followers were to be sent packing and the commanders of regiments were to be 'answerable that no rum, or spirits of any kind, be sold in or near the camp'. 'Any persons detected robbing the tents of officers or soldiers' would if condemned 'certainly be executed'. Any soldier found outside the camp lines or with 'plunder in his tent' was to be 'sent to the Provost in irons to be tried for his life'. Men who gave away or sold their rum allowances were warned that they ran the risk not only of being 'struck entirely out of the Roll when rum is delivered out' but also of being tried and sentenced by court martial.

The General was annoyed also with the results of some of the patrols sent out at this time to reconnoitre the country beyond the army's flanks. Major Scott, who took a patrol on 7 July six miles south of Monckton's camp on Pointe de Lévy as far as the Echemin River, which runs into the St Lawrence through thickly wooded country, thought it prudent to return when he was fired on by some Indians.

On presenting his report to Wolfe he was berated for his excessive caution, and losing his temper he threatened the General with a 'Parliamentary Enquiry for not consulting an inferior officer and seeming to disregard his sentiments'.

That evening Wolfe wrote contemptuously in his diary that 'some skattering shott from the woods and the sight of a few Indians had determined him to retire'.

The General was irritated not only by the lack of courage and resource shown by his officers, but also by what he took to be the careless inefficiency of the Navy. 'Disposition of the frigates and bomb ketches', he noted with laconic ill-temper in his diary two evenings later. 'Their prodigious distance from the enemy—amazing backwardness in these matters on the side of the Fleet.'

Above all he was angered by the waspish raids of the savages and Canadian settlers on his outposts, particularly those against the south flank of Monckton's brigade where the construction of the batteries was progressing with such frustrating slowness. He was sure that the troops were insufficiently alert and excessively nervous and warned them that 'any officer or N.C.O. who shall suffer himself to be surprised by the enemy, must not expect to be forgiven. False alarms are hurtful in an army, and dishonourable to those who occasion them. . . . In most attacks by night it must be remembered that bayonets are preferable to fire.'

The American rangers, who were sent out to harry these guerrillas, found it difficult to come to grips with the crafty, silent Abernakis Indians and generally succeeded only in killing or bringing in as prisoners a few Canadian farmers, old men or boys. One of these squads of rangers, raised in New England, was despatched on a fighting patrol to the south on 9 July and captured a boy of fifteen and a man of about forty with his two little sons. As they were bringing them back to the camp they were pursued by a group of Canadians and Indians, and the officer in command

71

of the rangers, anxious lest the howls of the young boys
should give his position away, tried at first to quiet them and
then to shoo them away. But in their fright they did not
understand his frantic gestures and one of the rangers
stepped forward and shot them both. Cruelties such as
these committed by both sides began to give to the campaign
an aspect of bitterness and sullen, revengeful anger. The
Canadians, imitating their Indian allies, scalped and
castrated English soldiers and American rangers whenever
they could get hold of a corpse or a badly wounded body,
while the Americans, and the British soldiers too, infected
by the violence, returned outrage for outrage without the
excuse of traditional custom. Sometimes when an Indian
was being scalped, blue and white war paint was rubbed off
to reveal the pale European features of a Canadian whose
white body, naked, without even what Townshend called
the Indian's 'arse-clout', was covered with a reddish-brown
dye. Although this habit of disguising themselves as
Indians and racing naked through the dark woods to kill
the enemy with tomahawks and scalping knives, deepened
the sensual thrill of violence, it also gave the British an
official excuse for scalping them should they be killed. For
Wolfe, who forbade his soldiers the use of the scalping knife,
expressly reserved from his order savages and 'Canadians
disguised as savages'. And any disguised Canadian who was
killed was scalped as a matter of course.

Impatient with the slow progress of the batteries at
Pointe de Lévy, Wolfe had for some days been preparing
plans for the erection of other batteries to fire against the
opposite flank of the enemy's position. By 9 July his plans
were ready and several frigates and a bomb ketch sailed out
towards the Montmorency cataract, to the west of which the
left flank of the French army was firmly entrenched. For the
whole day the ships lobbed shells up on to the cliff-top,
but the gunners were unable to maintain an accurate fire

with their shells, following so steep a trajectory. Many fell short and exploded against the cliff-face or were swallowed up in the roaring cataract itself, while others flew over the French lines and wasted their force in the fields and woods beyond them. The few that found their mark did little damage.

The ineffectual cannonade gave Lévis, who commanded the Canadian troops along the Montmorency River, ample warning of the English commander's intention, and although Monckton marched part of his brigade upstream along the banks of the St Lawrence towards the Echemin River the intended diversion was not sufficiently convincing to evoke the expected response. And at dusk the French could see the English troops drawn up on the shores of Ile d'Orléans and embarking in the landing-craft.

The whole of Townshend's and Murray's brigades embarked during the night and sailed towards the northern shore, leaving a detachment of marines under Major Hardy to hold the island.

The light infantry and the grenadiers were the first to land; and Wolfe, as always, directed the leading wave. The French had not thought it worth while opposing a landing that side of the Montmorency River with more than a few Canadians and Indians. And although these sharp-shooters caused several casualties as the troops disembarked on the unknown shore in the darkness, as soon as the landing of the first wave was completed they retired to the woods and left the light infantry free to climb the cliffs and en-trench themselves on the heights above.

Before dawn the second wave of troops, comprising most of the remaining three thousand men in the two brigades, had landed, and Townshend looked about at the landing-place for a guide to show him where the light infantry and grenadiers had climbed the cliff and the positions they were now occupying. But he could find no one. The first wave of troops seemed to have disappeared into the night. It was still

73

very dark and while it had been simple enough to get two companies of picked troops up the cliff it was a very different matter to get two heavy brigades and their artillery up without any help from those who had led the attack and should, Townshend thought with good cause, have made some effort to help him.

Eventually he found the baggage of the grenadiers and light infantry in a field near the shore, but there was no one with it to give him any orders, nor in fact to guard it from the Indians who might well have plundered it under cover of the darkness. Leaving an officer and twenty men to look after Wolfe's baggage and his own, he led the two brigades up on to the summit. As soon as the leading regiment was safely in position he sent a detachment back for the guns, and as dawn broke six six-pounders were dragged up on to the heights.

Giving orders for his men to entrench themselves as quickly as possible, Townshend went off to look for Wolfe in the gathering light. He discovered him occupying a position which he considered ludicrous, with his unprotected rear exposed to the woods on the high ground to the north. A few hours later, to Townshend's grim satisfaction, this ill-chosen position led to fourteen of Wolfe's men losing their scalps to an Indian raiding party.

Townshend found the General in an imperious mood. He told him that he had been remarkably slow in getting his two brigades up the cliffs and asked if he might enquire who had given Brigadier Townshend orders to make his position like a fortress from which the men could not possibly advance. Townshend replied that the men could leap over the fortification which they had made in 'an instant' and that in any case with so much timber lying about they had been able to make twenty yards of parapet in a quarter of an hour. 'With respect to his objection to the making my work like a fortress', Townshend wrote in his diary, 'I must observe he must have had an uncommon

74

disposition to find fault with me for making my work too strong in three hours' time!'

Wolfe brushed aside Townshend's excuses and completely altered the disposition of his units and the siting of his guns. He made three battalions, Townshend remembered, encamp 'upon the descent of the hill with their front to the River St Lawrence and their rear to the rear of our first line; exposed to the cannon shot of the enemy, the first of which went through their tents and raked their encampment from right to left'.

The General seemed, for the first time since they had arrived in Canada, almost happy. Tirelessly he moved about in the forward detachments, organizing patrols, siting batteries, peering through his telescope at the gaps between the trees. At last he was doing something, the enforced inactivity of the past few frustrating days was over and he had more important things to do than visit the slow-moving soldiers at Pointe de Lévy and issue orders about camp discipline. But what he hoped to achieve by bringing half his army to the banks of the Montmorency even he was not yet sure. If he could find a ford he might be able to get his troops across in sufficient force to attack the Canadians from the rear. But was there a ford? And even if there was how successful could he expect to be in getting his men through the Indian-infested woods which lined both sides of the river? And how well would his brave, well-trained, but sometimes unimaginative troops stand up to the Canadians, who—while they were, it is true, no match for them in the regular fighting and open ground warfare for which the British soldier had been trained—had had years of experience of fighting under cover and in the forest?

According to Wolfe's journal, the landing at Montmorency had originally been planned as a feint for a landing nearer Quebec. But that scheme was now abandoned, and the Montmorency camp was to remain his headquarters for nearly two months.

75

During these two months the most that Wolfe could hope for was that by flanking fire from new batteries he might make the enemy entrenchments untenable, and that by dividing his forces in this way he might tempt Montcalm to attack him while relying on the Navy to get his troops across the river to the threatened spot before the men defending it were overwhelmed. If Montcalm attacked him in force across the Montmorency he could get Monckton back from Pointe de Lévy while he delayed the battle in the open country to the east of the river; if Monckton were to be attacked, the Navy could rush Townshend's and Murray's brigades back to help him; and if Ile d'Orléans were threatened the whole army could return to defeat the French there. In any event he was sure that once he could get the French army to move he could defeat them.

Lévis, on the other hand, was equally certain that he could cross the Montmorency and attack and defeat Wolfe before the rest of the English army had time to come to his rescue. Montcalm thought this quite possible, but saw no point in taking the risk. He doubted that Wolfe would be so reckless as to attack him through the woods. In any case the only ford was a good three miles upstream and that was well defended by over a thousand Canadians under a reliable French officer. And even if the English did manage to get a dangerous force across the river and through the ambush-silent woods, there was a line of strongly fortified stone farm buildings and cottages joined by deep entrenchments to face them when they came out into the open. It was not Wolfe who worried Montcalm, but Amherst far away in the south, who might take Ticonderoga and advance up the shores of Lake Champlain to capture Montreal and thus threaten his rear. Wolfe, the reckless 'joueur', alarmed him not at all by this latest gambit. Drive Wolfe and his two brigades away, he told Lévis, 'and they will be troublesome somewhere else. While they are there they cannot do much harm. So let them amuse themselves.'

The English soldiers found their duties far from amusing. Every day reconnaissance patrols were sent into the woods under Mohawk guides to search for a ford, and working-parties protected by rangers were ordered in to cut fascines for the batteries. The soldiers hated going into the woods, where their bright uniforms were so clear a target, and dreaded the fall of night and the long hours of darkness surrounded by a silent, watchful enemy.

The skill of the Indians in tracking and killing their prey was described by Sergeant Johnson of the 58th.

As soon as the Victim is within their aim [he wrote] they Fire, and very often kill him dead on the Spot; for they very seldom miss their aim, being excellent marksmen; however that be, they immediately spring up to him, and with their Butt strike at his head and endeavour to beat out his brains.—If upon their advance towards him, they discover any Signs of resistance, they again take shelter, as near the Victim as possible, and then taking a cool and deliberate Aim, they throw their Tomma Hawk, an instrument made in the shape of our camp hatchets; the head not quite so large with a sharp turn on the back of the head, resembling a hawk's bill, and a longer handle, but not so thick as our Camp hatchets; which they throw with great certainty for a considerable distance and seldom miss; no sooner have they delivered the Tomma hawk out of their hand, but they spring up to him, with their Scalping Knife; which is made in every respect like our Kitchen Carving Knives, and generally at the first approach rip him open, and sometimes take out his heart, but not always; it often happens that time won't permit to perpetrate that barbarous part of their inhuman cruelty.—After all they cut round the top of the crown, to the Skull bone, and raising up one Side the Skin, with the Knife, with a jerk they tear it off by the hair, and the work is done; upon which they set up the Indian Whoop, as a signal to their barbarous companions that the work is finished, as also a Shout of Triumph.

One day a band of four hundred Indians crept up on a large working-party collecting fascines in the woods. The Canadian officer in command of the Indians sent back a message that the English were at their mercy. On receipt of the message Lévis sent to Vaudreuil for instructions. Vaudreuil told him to do nothing until he arrived. But it was not until two hours later that Vaudreuil, terrified by the thought of making a wrong decision, arrived at Lévis's headquarters. And by then it was too late. The Indians, tired of waiting, had stood up and fired on the American guards. The Americans retreated in good order on the infantrymen, who, given good warning this time of the Indians' presence, snatched their muskets and held their ground. After an hour's lively firing from both sides the Indians were driven off, but they carried nearly forty scalps back to their wigwams with them, giving Wolfe further evidence that, even when not surprised, his soldiers needed more experience of backwoods fighting before they could hope to meet the Canadians or Indians on equal terms in the forest.

The soldiers, aware of this, began to teach themselves new tactics and to learn from experience how to combat the Indian's quick mind. Having a traditional and inbred horror of being worsted in a fight or in an argument, they soon realized that more than stolid courage and determined discipline was required in this strange country. They imitated Lord Howe's light infantry and, so far as their officers would allow them to, they modified their uniforms to suit the background against which they fought. They tied up their coat-tails, turned their coats inside out, and rubbed camouflaging mud into the linings, spread queue grease on their musket barrels to take the shine off them, and stuck twigs into their button-holes and leaves into their hats. Instead of marching their men through the woods in orderly files, the officers and sergeants spread them out in loose formation and made them dart from tree to tree. The English, the Indians complained with admiring surprise, no longer stood still to be shot at. Night after night soldiers in twos and threes crept out into the woods to lie in ambush and to try to earn the five guineas reward which Wolfe promised any man who caught an Indian dead or alive.

With this newly found confidence the troops began to find life more enjoyable. The nights in the outposts were still dreaded, but since three single sentries had been carried off to be mutilated by Indians a recent Order had made it compulsory for all posts to be manned by at least two men. And the posts themselves were now placed nearer the tents of the guard. Molasses became a pleasant addition to the daily rations, and rum was plentiful—on some days each man got a full gill measure. Occasionally the rain fell in torrential bursts, flooding the trenches and swamping the tents, but more often the air was dry and warm and the sun shone brightly. Bathing was forbidden in the heat of the day, but in the early morning and after five o'clock in the evening the soldiers ran naked across the sandy flats east of the roaring waterfall and threw themselves gratefully into the sparkling river.

On 14 July the men were delighted to hear that the General Orders permitted 'regiments and corps to send to Point of Orleans for one woman per company'. This was more like the sort of life they had enlisted for.

8

THE gradual improvement in spirits was not universal. The General himself was restless and irritable again. He had not brought his soldiers over the river, he told one of them, merely for their own enjoyment; and now that it was obvious that the French were not going to attack him and that he could not attack them from his new position, he was anxiously looking for fresh opportunities and a different position from which to make an assault.

'No man', Captain Knox noted in his journal, 'can display greater activity than he does.' He was more ubiquitous than ever. One day he would be in the farm cottage near the Montmorency cataract which he had occupied as his headquarters, the next he would be with Monckton on Pointe de Lévy. During the morning of 12 July an officer in the 58th Regiment saw him inspecting a forward post near Beaumont, two hours later he was on board a frigate four miles away.

Townshend found him quite impossible. He would never discuss anything of importance with him or in fact with any of his senior officers. He never asked for counsel and resented the advice of anyone who ventured to make a suggestion.

One day Townshend heard that the General was just about to embark for Ile d'Orléans. Townshend, who had not been told either that the General was leaving or when he would be back, rushed down to the water's edge for the orders which, as Wolfe's second-in-command at Montmorency, he felt should be given him.

He received me in a very stately manner, [Townshend wrote in his diary] not advancing five steps. I told him that if I had suspected his intention of going over I had waited on him for his commands which I should be glad to receive and execute to his satisfaction. 'Sir', said he dryly, 'the Adjutant-General has my orders—permit me, sir, to ask are your troops to encamp on the new ground or not to do it until the enemy's battery begins to play?'

And with this rhetorical question and implied rebuke he stepped into the boat and was rowed off to Ile d'Orléans, calling on the way to visit Admiral Saunders, whom he had also offended by some harshly critical remarks about the 'irregularities committed by the seamen' and their failure to protect the troops against the enemy's floating batteries and gun-boats.

Wolfe's dislike of Townshend had recently been increased by an unfortunate incident in the mess. Asked to entertain the officers with his famous caricatures, Townshend had drawn a derisively bawdy picture of the General building a line of entrenchments round a brothel. The cartoon was so outrageously funny that each officer to whom it was passed roared with laughter at the sight of it. Eventually it was passed to the General by an officer who thought that he too would be amused by it. Wolfe looked at it and his face went deathly pale. He crumpled the paper up and put it into his pocket. 'If we live', he said, looking at Townshend, 'this shall be enquired into.'

On 12 July the anxious General was given some encouragement by the long-awaited news that Monckton's batteries on Pointe de Lévy were completed. At nine o'clock a rocket was fired into the darkening sky and the cannons at last roared into life. Both the first and the second salvo of shells fell short, and the triumphantly disdainful shouts of the French garrison could be heard across the river. Within a few minutes, however, the gunners had found the range and the shells could be seen bursting on the wharves and in the streets of the Lower Town and some against the stone walls of the Upper Town itself. All night long the cannonade furiously continued and was as furiously returned. For two months the bombardment was to be carried on with only brief intervals of quiet while the guns were cleaned or supplies of ammunition momentarily ran out. On 15 July a shell set fire to a wooden building in the Upper Town, and a high north-west wind carried the fire to the cathedral, which was itself also hit by a shell that same night and was burned to the ground within the hour. A week later the strong wind came up again, and a fierce fire in the Lower Town demolished many of the wooden sheds and warehouses down by the river's edge.

Life in the constantly bombarded town became unbearable for those who had no compelling reason to remain, and day after day the rough and narrow roads leading out of it were choked with wagons and carriages on their way out to the safety of the country or south to Montreal. Deserters and prisoners told the same anguished story. A bag of letters captured by a fighting patrol made pitiful reading. 'The English are too cunning for us', a priest had written to a friend, 'and who would have thought it? They have made this town so hot that there is but one place left, where we can with safety pay adoration to our once Gracious but now wrathful and displeased God, who we much fear has forsaken us.'

'I herewith send you', another letter ran, 'fourteen biscuits which are all that I can spare and in our present distressed and most deplorable situation are quite a compliment I assure you.'

On cold nights, in their uncomfortable entrenchments, the soldiers on guard could look towards Quebec and watch with malicious pleasure the flashes and flying sparks, the tongues of flame and crumbling masonry, which told them of the slow destruction of a once lovely town.

As the long weeks of July wore on some such evidence of the enemy's discomfiture was sadly needed. Since the

General had taken Townshend's and Murray's brigades to the banks of the Montmorency the operations seemed to be at a standstill.

The Navy, it is true, had succeeded, with much difficulty owing to unfavourable winds, in getting several ships past the batteries at Quebec into the upper river and had attacked some fireships and provision boats west of the town. And this had forced Montcalm to send nine hundred men under Dumas to defend the river line between Quebec and Cap Rouge should the English try to land there. But the threat did not seem a serious one, nor did Montcalm appear unduly concerned by the movement of troops and landing-craft along the southern banks of the river which followed it. He took it to be a bait, which it was, and he did not rise to it. With these troops on the southern bank detached from the three main camps on Pointe de Lévy, Ile d'Orléans, and along the Montmorency River, Wolfe had split his army into four in the hope that Montcalm would attack him; but the French general watched and waited and stayed where he was.

The French indeed were more alarmed by the activities of the fleet than of the army, and in an effort to destroy Saunders's ships they prepared for another attack with fire-craft. Towards the end of the month they were ready and awaited a favourable wind. They had schooners, shallops, and floating stages chained together in a line over two hundred yards long. Every vessel was loaded with grape-shot, barrels of powder packed with bits of metal, grenades and broken guns. On the evening of 27 July a strong wind came up and the Canadian crews jumped aboard the deserted, ghost-like decks.

The line of fireships cast off and slowly sailed across the dark river. Halfway across, the order to fire the ships was given and torches were plunged into tar barrels and trains of powder crackled over the decks towards the unmanned guns in the stern. A few seconds later it seemed, one soldier thought, as if a volcano had erupted beneath the river bed. The noise of shells and grenades exploding, and the roaring of guns filled the air, while the sky was a golden red with the continuously raging fires and bursts of rioting sparks.

As the alarm rang out on the British ships, the sailors tumbled out of their hammocks and dashed on deck. Without waiting for any further command, they slipped overboard, most of them still in their underclothes and stockinged feet, and jumped into the boats. Rushing down to the river's edge, the soldiers saw them, with chains and ropes round their necks and grappling-hooks in their hands, throwing lines round the crackling, roaring ships, undoing the tangled chains, slashing at ropes, and laughingly towing the dangerous craft away as calmly and confidently as they had done the month before. 'Damme, Jack', an officer heard one sailor shout to another in real enjoyment, 'did ye ever take hell in tow before?'

Wolfe took a sterner view of the episode. 'If the enemy presume', he told them in an angry note sent over to Quebec under a flag of truce the following day, 'to send down any more firecrafts, they are to be made fast to two particular transports in which are all the Canadians and other prisoners in order that they may perish by their own base inventions.'

To keep the troops occupied during the stalemated days of July, and to bring in prisoners and information, the General sent out fighting patrols deep into Canadian territory. Colonel Carleton was sent eighteen miles upriver with a large harassing patrol of six hundred men to make a raid on Pointe-aux-Trembles, and returned with a bundle of private correspondence and nearly two hundred prisoners, mostly women, old men, and children, refugees from Quebec.

The more presentable women were invited to dinner by the General Staff, and the General himself joined them.

84

He could not understand the attitude of the French command, he told one of them : 'I have given them good chances to attack me and am surprised they have not profited by them.'

Other raiding parties, less elaborate than Colonel Carleton's, were more successful. One of the most rewarding was led by Major Dalling on 25 July, when not only 250 Canadian prisoners were taken, but also more than twice as many horses, sheep, lambs, and cows.

For the duties of these fighting patrols had been extended. They were now scouring and ravaging parties also. On 23 July a second proclamation had been issued to the Canadian people, in which they were informed that the General was 'offended by the little regard that the inhabitants of Canada had paid to his former proclamation'. They were 'unworthy' of the previous offer made to them. Raiding parties were to 'burn and lay waste the country for the future, sparing only churches or houses dedicated to divine worship'. Women and children were not to be harmed, but otherwise the officers in command were given a free hand.

Constant complaints were made by Wolfe against the atrocities committed by the Canadians and Indians as if he wished by emphasizing these atrocities to make his own depredations the more excusable. The correspondence between Wolfe and Vaudreuil became more and more acrimonious. Vaudreuil replied to Wolfe's angry complaints about the inhumanities of the French and Canadians with instances of atrocities committed by English and American patrols. The former polite tone of the notes taken across the river by canoes flying their flags of truce had now completely vanished.

During the earlier days of July women prisoners captured by fighting patrols had been returned to Quebec under the courteous protection of an aide-de-camp; Wolfe had presented Vaudreuil with a dozen bottles of rum; the

Canadian Governor had politely returned the compliment with a case of wine. But these pleasant formalities were now abruptly discontinued. It was quite obvious, Vaudreuil wrote, after a consignment of female prisoners had been paddled across the St Lawrence and escorted to Quebec, that the English parade of generosity in returning unarmed civilians to their homes was merely prompted by an inability to feed them. Wolfe replied that in view of the Governor's comments no further prisoners would, in any circumstances, be returned.

When three grenadiers were captured by Indians Wolfe sent a note to Vaudreuil protesting that he had heard that they were to be burned alive. Vaudreuil coldly replied that the grenadiers had, in accordance with the usual humane custom of the Canadian authorities, been ransomed at the expense of the King of France. Wolfe, however, professed himself unsatisfied, and the proclamation to the Canadians was put into effect with extreme thoroughness. Every night patrols brought in quantities of cattle and supplies and left the countryside through which they passed a burning wilderness.

When not engaged in raids, the men were kept busy with less adventurous duties. They were brought back from forward posts for inspections, drill parades, and the constant musketry practice which the General considered of such importance. A new method of 'pushing bayonets' was taught throughout the army and was considered ludicrously stupid. Captain Knox, watching the men practise it, thought they looked like a lot of 'indolent haymakers'. Different methods of landing from floating stages were tried out, and the infantrymen spent long hours constructing and testing new models designed by the Chief Engineer. The largest type was designed to carry three hundred men and was kept above water by rum casks fastened together with cables. There was a handrail to three sides, and the fourth was protected by a musket-proof fence which was let down on landing.

Despite their constant activity the troops, after their short period of cheerfulness in the warm July sunshine, began to grow restless and discontented again. Towards the end of the month the skies clouded over and the sultry air became oppressive with the threat of rain. The men had to be reminded 'in the strongest manner' of the importance of keeping their camps 'sweet and clean' and of burying their 'offal and filth'. General Orders specified the making of 'new Necessary Houses at least every third day'. The women were told that if they persisted in selling liquor and getting the men drunk they would be put back in the holds of the ships. One woman sutler was drummed along the lines for keeping what the General referred to as a 'disorderly tent'. A Regimental Order deplored the 'constant swearing and indecent language used amongst men such as is unbecoming gentlemen and soldiers', and company commanders were desired to 'confine any man so offending'. The first deserters began to swim across the river to give themselves up to a more cheerful life behind the French lines.

Conscious that the stalemated campaign was largely responsible for the lowering spirits of the men, Wolfe pondered ceaselessly on the possibilities of attack. He had done everything he could to make Montcalm attack him, and now, however dangerous it seemed, he must attack Montcalm. But where? Along the whole wide front there was no possible point for an attack where the cliffs were less than a hundred feet above the water.

At attack on the northern shore above Quebec was suggested. He had already considered this. Indeed, an attack here had occupied his mind ever since the beginning of the month, when the British occupation of Pointe de Lévy had made it easier for ships to slip past Quebec into the upper river. On 3 July he had spoken to Saunders of the possibility of getting 'ashore above the town'. And two days later Murray had reported that he thought a landing could be made at Sillery. The idea of a landing there or nearer

Quebec was still in his mind when Wolfe took the troops across the St Lawrence to the banks of the Montmorency on 9 July. But during the next week something happened to change his plans. On 19 July he noted in his journal, 'reconnoitred the country immediately above Quebec and found that if we had ventured the stroke that was first intended we should probably have succeeded'. The next day he made a reconnaissance higher up, past Sillery and as far as Cap Rouge. Why he left it until 19 July to make this personal inspection is obscure. He implied in his despatch to

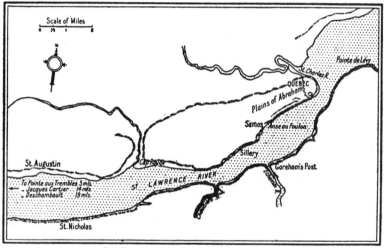

St Lawrence River above Quebec

Pitt that it was not possible for him to do so until some of the larger ships got into the upper river, and this did not take place until two men-of-war and two armed sloops got past Quebec on 18 July. But Murray had been as far upstream as Sillery almost a fortnight before. In any case Wolfe decided now against an attack on any part of the northern coast above Quebec, giving as his reasons the fear that 'the body first landed could not be reinforced before they were attacked by the enemy's whole army' and the knowledge

88

that the 'enemy were jealous of the design' and 'preparing against it'. On 23 July he was making plans for an attack on the Beauport shore north of Ile d'Orléans.

It was to be a frontal assault against the very heart of the enemy position. The boldness of it alarmed the brigadiers and the senior naval officers, who confessed themselves unable to hope for much chance of success. But Wolfe was adamant. Something must be done. This was it.

The actual point of attack was to be a mile upstream from the gorge of the Montmorency cataract, where there was a strand of dry land between the bottom of the cliff and the edge of the river. At high tide this strand was about two hundred yards wide, and as the waters fell with the ebbing tide they left beyond the dry strand a waste of rivulet-cleft mud which stretched for half a mile towards the now narrow channel of the river. On the strand the French had built two gun emplacements, and there were others towards the Beauport battery in front of Montcalm's headquarters.

These emplacements were commanded by the entrench-ments on the cliff above, so that to attack them was bound to be an extremely hazardous undertaking. Wolfe hoped, however, that a heavy and continuous bombardment, both from his camp at Montmorency and from ships in the river, would force the despised Canadians to retreat from their entrenchments, or would at least keep them quiet, while his men captured the gun emplacements on the strand. What he expected to do afterwards is not clear. To attempt to scale the cliffs in broad daylight would have been suicidal, to expect the French to come down and fight on the strand an absurd assessment of the enemy's ability. That he was expecting a heavy engagement was obvious from the numbers of troops involved.

Two thousand men under Townshend were to ford the Montmorency at the foot of the cataract at low tide and advance along the northern shore under the shadow of the cliffs, while another two thousand men under Wolfe and Monckton were to land on the mud flats and attack the French redoubts from the front. Cover was to be provided by the guns beyond the Montmorency River, by the batteries on Pointe de Lévy, and by a frigate anchored in midstream and two catamarans which were to sail as close as they could get to the French redoubts and allow themselves to sink into the mud as the tide receded. The men in the boats were to be protected as far as possible by the guns of the *Pembroke*, the *Trent*, the *Lowestoft* and the *Racehorse*.

The attack was to be made on 31 July.

9

IN the middle of the morning when the tide was at full flood, the *Centurion*, a sixty-four-gun frigate commanded by Captain Mantle, sailed slowly into the north channel towards the Beauport coast and anchored near the gorge of the Montmorency River. As the anchor settled down on to the rocky bed of the St Lawrence, the ship's guns opened up in a furious cannonade on the redoubts at the edge of the strand, beneath the overhanging cliffs.

It was the signal for an intense bombardment. The *Centurion's* guns rolled and boomed at the French entrenchments, and the two catamarans, each with fourteen guns, tacked in as close as they could get to the redoubt nearest the Montmorency River and soon their guns too were flashing and smoking in the warm sunlight. As the ships in the river fired continuously at the redoubts on the strand, a battery of nearly fifty heavy pieces in the camp at Montmorency bombarded the French positions along the clifftop, while the battery at Pointe de Lévy cannonaded them from across the St Lawrence basin. For two hours the thunderous bombardment continued while the troops who had been in the landing-craft since ten o'clock waited, hot, cramped, and sweating, for the attack to begin.

About two o'clock some of the landing-craft moved out into midstream and the sailors rowed them up and down in front of the Beauport coast in an attempt to mislead the French commanders as to their landing-place.

Montcalm and Lévis, however, were not in any doubt as to where the attack was intended. Already the Canadians on the threatened heights, standing up well under the heavy fire from which they were partly protected by well-constructed traverses, had been reinforced by three regular French battalions and some heavy pieces of artillery which had been moved east from the village of Beauport. By five o'clock more than eleven thousand men were concentrated along the three and a half miles of cliff-top between Beauport church and the waterfall, while along the Montmorency River, in case of a secondary attack in their rear, five hundred more men were posted in the woods.

The day was still excessively hot, but the sun was now hidden behind low, dark clouds and the air was sultry and heavy. The tide was ebbing, and the catamarans stranded by the falling water were stuck securely in the silt as they kept up their fire against the redoubts.

In the early afternoon, when the tide was running low and the long stretch of dark mud along the river's edge was almost a quarter of a mile wide, Wolfe gave the order to attack.

The sailors rowed the unwieldy landing-craft across the narrowing channel towards the French redoubts. Wolfe, standing, cane in hand, in one of the leading boats, peered ahead at the landing-place as the sailors struggled to keep the boats from being washed too far downstream in the rushing currents. All the boats in the first wave, containing three companies of grenadiers and a detachment of Royal Americans, were swept too far downstream and grounded on ridges of mud, where, as the sailors struggled to release them, they made an easy target for French and Canadian sharpshooters on the cliffs above.

Some boats got free and slipped into deeper channels as others became more securely embedded in the silt. The *Centurion* and the two catamarans increased their rate of fire as the French batteries opened up with telling effect on the tightly packed men in the stranded boats.

Wolfe, shouting orders from his boat, was three times struck by splinters and had his cane knocked out of his hand by a round shot. Deciding that it was impossible to get the boats in any closer to the dry sand, he told Captain Hervey Smith, his aide-de-camp, to go to Townshend and tell him to halt his men as the landing of the first troops had been delayed. He realized now that he must wait until the tide was at its lowest before he could get his men ashore. Some of them had now been nearly eight hours in the crowded boats, and they waited impatiently for the order to get out.

While they were waiting a Captain David Ochterlony, who was in command of the detachment of the 60th and who had been wounded the day before in a duel with a German officer, Captain Wetterstroom of the grenadiers, saw Wetterstroom in a nearby boat. Standing up he shouted at him, 'Though my men are not grenadiers, you will see we shall be first at the redoubt.' The grenadiers roared back their defiance, and a moment or two later Wolfe gave the order for the boats to get in as close as they could to the strand and for the men to disembark.

The men of the 60th and the grenadiers, cheered by the sailors in the landing craft, raced each other across the slippery mud, in wild disorder, excited and uncontrollable, towards the redoubt at the edge of the dry sand. The French defenders of it, seeing their fierce, lumbering advance of nearly a thousand men, abandoned it; and a minute or two later the British were in possession.

No sooner, however, had their own troops got out of range than the French on the heights above rained down a furious fire of musket shot on the heads of the disorderly British soldiers, who could not with any hope of success reply to it.

Behind them the scene was chaotic. Monckton was already landing the second wave of troops, Amherst's Regiment and Fraser's Highlanders, a thousand men in all; while Townshend's two thousand men were already across the ford. No one knew what was expected of him. Now that

93

the French were obviously not coming down to fight, what was to be done? Nobody knew. The orders previously given to the grenadiers, to form up in four sections and await the arrival of the second wave of troops and Townshend's brigade, were now plainly unworkable. But no other instructions were given them. As the officers waited indecisively for orders the rain began to drizzle down.

In those few minutes of doubt the grenadiers decided for themselves what the next step should be. They had had enough hanging about for one day. Eight hours cramped up in a boat in the sweltering heat was enough to try anyone's patience. They knew where the enemy were so they thought they might as well get at them. Without waiting for orders from the General, or it seems from their own officers, they dashed across the strand, shouting at the top of their voices, and began to clamber up the steep and slippery cliff, encouraged by a solitary drummer who stood below them wildly beating his drum. The ascent was extremely difficult. The boots of the grenadiers slipped and slithered on the loose stones and shale and on the wet earth. Here and there, there was a bush to cling to or the root of a stunted cedar or hazel tree, but most of the surface of the brown cliff was bare and smooth; and higher up it was made more difficult to climb by the easily dislodged trunks of barkless trees which the enemy had put across the small ravines where the going would otherwise have been easier.

The soldiers struggled up, some with their muskets slung across their backs, others grimly holding them in one hand as they clawed at the earth with the other; but none of them able to return the fire of the French from the crest of the hill above them. Their officers, forced into the mad assault by the enthusiasm of their men and wondering what else, in any case, the General could have intended them to do, were now determined to make it successful. They encouraged the men with shouts and gestures to get to the top of the cliff while their desperate energy lasted.

The French and Canadians, delighted to have so perfect a target and, having suffered very few losses during the day's bombardment thanks to their well-made defences, shot carefully aimed volleys of musket balls down the slope and tilted up the breeches of their cannon to such an angle that the barrels were pointing sharply down the line of the cliff.

Despite the storm of shot and ball, lead and splinters, the grenadiers and Royal Americans struggled on, more slowly now as they became short of breath and their arms and legs grew weak with exhaustion. Soldier after soldier stumbled and fell in the smoke and then rolled down the cliff face until stopped by a ledge of earth, a tree trunk, or another soldier still clambering breathlessly upwards.

And then the black clouds, which all that sultry afternoon had been growing more heavy, suddenly broke and the rain poured blindingly down. Within a few minutes the cliff face became a morass. The grenadiers, soaked to the skin, could no longer see the top of the cliff through the sheets of slanting rain ; their powder became sodden, their muskets unusable. They were forced back at last, and in a slithering, tumbling mass they slipped and slid down the cliff like ants washed down the slopes of an ant-hill. Behind them hundreds of sprawled bodies, their red-and-white uniforms coated with mud, could be seen through the storm. Some of the wounded, too weak to hold on any longer or losing their footholds in the now slushy earth, rolled over and over in agony to the bottom of the cliff.

The French, until then shouting '*Vive le Roi!*' in triumphant excitement, fell silent as they looked down at the havoc which they and the storm had wrought. It was a piteous and subduing sight ; and as if to emphasize its horror the rain then stopped as abruptly as it had begun, and the cliff face, litered with sodden corpses, steamed in the sudden silence.

As the retreat was sounded, groups of Indians, their

scalping knives clenched between their teeth, scrambled down the cliff side to scalp the dead and wounded.

Lieutenant Henry Peyton of the Royal Americans, although badly wounded in the legs, sat up against a rock, where he had found a pouch of dry powder and fired at these scalping parties. David Ochterlony, who lay near him now mortally wounded in the lungs, was approached by one band. Peyton shot and killed two of the leading Indians and the others slunk off to other bodies less well protected.

By now Fraser's Highlanders were on shore fighting the Indians for possession of the wounded bodies and dragging off as many as they could across the mud flats to the waiting boats.

A tough sergeant of the Highlanders came up to Lieutenant Peyton and offered to take him off to the boats, but he refused to leave his friend Ochterlony, who was dying and who begged not to be carried away from the scene of so humiliating a disaster. An hour later, when the evacuation was almost completed, a Frenchman and two Indians crept up behind the British officers. The Frenchman snatched Peyton's laced hat from his head and robbed Ochterlony of his watch and money. Then one of the Indians tried to strangle Ochterlony with his sash while the other stabbed him in the stomach with his scalping knife. Peyton who had by now been able to load again, shot one of the Indians and killed him. The other lunged at him with a bayonet which went into his side. As the Indian was trying to pull it out, Peyton grabbed the scalping knife which dangled from his belt and stabbed him in the back. A few moments later a French soldier came up and threatened to shoot the next Indian who attacked the wounded officers ; and then picking up the scarcely conscious Ochterlony, he carried him off to the General Hospital in Quebec, where, shortly afterwards, he died. Lieutenant Peyton, now no longer having any reason to stay, agreed to be carried off and Captain Mac-Donald slung him across his shoulders and took him back to the river's edge.

The French watched the evacuation from the cliff-top, taking no action to prevent it. Their ammunition had been ruined by the storm and in any event they were in no mood to add further horrors to the scene of slaughter. Some of their officers came down to do what they could to prevent the Indians butchering the wounded and walked about on the strand, inspecting the evacuation as though on an exercise, talking to the grenadiers and Highlanders, and watching the straggling groups of soldiers with their limp and heavy burdens dripping water and blood into the sand.

It was as if the war were already over. The guns on both sides were silent.

IO

LATER on that evening, looking down to the St
Lawrence and the stranded boats scuttled and
burning, Vaudreuil was in cheerful and contented
mood. 'I have', he told Bourlamaque, who commanded the
French army in the south, 'no more anxiety about Quebec.
Wolfe, I assure you, will make no progress. . . . He contented himself with losing about five hundred of his best
soldiers. Deserters say he will try again in a few days. That
is what we want ; he'll find out who he's talking to.'

The British defeat had certainly been severe, and the
officers of Wolfe's headquarters who dined with him at
Montmorency that night said that he seemed utterly stunned
by it. He had lost 443 men killed and wounded, including
33 officers, and had not killed a single Frenchman. He
had also given his senior officers further cause to doubt that
he was up to the task which Pitt had set him. Even the
impatient Murray, by no means a cautious man, was
known to have spoken of the attack as stupid and foolhardy. Townshend's criticisms were predictably harsh ; and
Monckton for once shaken out of his quiet loyalty, agreed
with Vaudreuil in considering the whole operation 'a mad
enterprise', certain to fail. 'An attack then and there', an
unusually outspoken staff officer wrote, 'was contrary to the
advice and opinion of every officer. And when things are
come to this, you'll judge what the event may be.' Like
Vaudreuil, the General's staff had no idea of what he had
hoped to gain by his attack.

His despatch to Pitt did not enlighten them. Nor did the
advantages of an attack at this point, which he listed in the

despatch, seem very convincing. He pointed out that here alone the artillery from the camp at Montmorency could effectively be used in support of the attack, that the whole British force could be used at once, and that there was an open way for retreat should that be necessary. 'Neither one or other of these advantages', he wrote, 'can anywhere else be found.' It was a sweeping statement, which, to say the least, was misleading. And his excuse that he could not see, until it was too late to turn back, that the French redoubts on the strand were within musket shot of the entrenchments on the cliffs above was strangely disingenuous.

He sent a copy of the draft of his despatch to Saunders, who returned it with a strong complaint that it gave to the Navy an unfair share of the blame for the failure. In a long and pitiful letter Wolfe replied that he would take out the part of the letter which Saunders objected to, 'although', he contended, 'the matter of fact to the best of my recollection is strictly as I have stated it. I am sensible of my own errors in the course of the campaign; see clearly wherein I have been deficient; and think a little more or less blame to a person who must necessarily be ruined of little or no consequence. . . . My ill state of health', he added, 'hinders me from executing my own plan.' But what that plan was he did not say. It was too desperate, he thought, to trust to the execution of others. But it could scarcely have been more desperate than the plans he was later to propose.

In the grenadiers he had a more blameworthy scapegoat than the Navy, and he was not prepared to accept responsibility for their part in the disaster. In a General Order which appeared the following morning his anger of the night before was apparent.

The check which the grenadiers met with yesterday [he wrote] will, it is hoped, be a lesson to them for the time to come; such *impetuous*, *irregular*, and *unsoldierlike* proceedings destroy all order, make it impossible for their commanders to form any disposition for an attack, and put it out of the General's power to execute his plan. The grenadiers should not suppose that they could beat the French army alone. . . . The very first fire of the enemy was sufficient to repulse men who had lost all sense of order and military discipline. . . . After this day the men are to begin work at six o'clock in the morning.

His anger and depression found other outlets. Two days after the publication of this philippic a third proclamation was issued to the Canadians, in which they were informed that the General's patience was exhausted and that as they continued to practise 'the most unchristian barbarities against his troops on all occasions he could no longer refrain from chastising them as they deserved'.

The threat of the proclamation was put into execution with spirit. Once more the people of Quebec looking out across the fields along the southern banks of the river could see farmsteads, haystacks, and crops burning fiercely and sending showers of sparks into the dark sky. These attacks on the Canadian *canaille*, the 'vermin' of the countryside were no longer incidental to the main tasks of reconnaissance or fighting patrols. They were tasks in themselves. Large detachments of light infantry, American rangers and sometimes regiments of the line were sent out nightly with no other object than to lay waste the settlements or villages in a specified area. Some of the detachments were sent as far down river as the Ile aux Coudres to ravage the settlements on the river banks beyond it, as a punishment to the Canadians for firing on the sounding-boats six weeks before. Others were sent as far to the south as the River Chaudière. Most of them carried out their orders with thoroughness, however much they may have regretted them. Some indeed performed their duties with apparent relish.

One of these, sent to the little village of St Joachim to the west of the Montmorency River, under command of Captain Alexander Montgomery of the 43rd Regiment, announced before departure its determination not to take any prisoners.

It occupied a house in the village close to one fortified and defended by the village priest and about eighty of his flock. Soon after his arrival Captain Montgomery received a friendly invitation to dinner from the priest, who suggested that he also bring along 'any officer of his detachment who would be kind enough to accompany him'.

Not knowing what to make of the invitation, the English officer ignored it and the next day he attacked the priest's house in force. His detachment was large and well trained and included several American rangers disguised as Indians. The priest thought it prudent to surrender to this formidable force and came out of the house followed by his parishioners.

Captain Montgomery, true to his promise, ordered every man to be shot. Some of them by this time were kneeling in prayer or supplication, but all of them were killed, and, according to the unreliable evidence of an English orderly sergeant who had deserted to the French after killing one of his officers, most of them were afterwards scalped. The priest himself was slashed to the ground with repeated sword strokes and when lying there he was scalped and his skull was smashed into the earth. His parish was burned to the ground.

The official reason given for this savage warfare against civilians, by eighteenth-century standards a novel interpretation of military rights, was that it would starve Quebec and induce the Canadian militia defending it to desert in order to protect their homes and families. It had little such effect. Most of Quebec's supplies came down the river from Montreal and from the countryside to the west, and, while conditions were bad enough in the besieged town, the burning of the harvest around the British army did not make them appreciably worse. As for the militia, the French had threatened to set the Indians on their families if they deserted, and so, accepting the sincerity of the threat and preferring an English death to an Indian one, most of them had already decided to stay.

Wolfe, restless and exhausted, his mind constantly at work with the problem of getting to grips with the enemy, had soon realized that Montcalm was not going to come down to fight him for the sake of a few scattered farms, and that if all the farms in the neighbourhood were to be destroyed Quebec would still be there unconquered.

Something more would have to be done to try to stop French supplies getting through from Trois Rivières and Montreal. Since the middle of July several more ships had got past the raging batteries at Quebec, but the flotilla beyond the town was still a small one and French store-ships were still slipping through. It was decided that the number of ships in the upper river must be increased, and a meeting was held at Wolfe's headquarters to discuss the matter.

It was agreed that by every favourable wind and tide a ship should slip up river, running the gauntlet past the guns in Quebec until a fleet of fair size had collected beyond the town. Although the St Lawrence is over a mile wide south-west of Quebec, it was hoped that many French ships might be intercepted sailing down from Montreal. This fleet, when assembled beyond Quebec, was to be put under the command of Admiral Holmes.

While these naval operations were in progress, Brigadier Murray with twelve hundred men was to march along the southern bank of the river beyond Pointe de Lévy and embark his men in flat-bottomed boats at a spot known as Goreham's Post. From here and other points of departure he was to make lightning raids on French outposts and commissaries, burning stores and taking prisoners.

On 6 August Murray, delighted at last to have a clear and definite duty, marched off. And on the same day two of Holmes's frigates shot past the batteries at Quebec, untouched and with flags flying bravely in the strong wind.

It seemed a good omen, and Wolfe needed some encouragement.

He was depressed and disconsolate. Since his quarrel with Saunders his relations with the Navy had been less friendly, and Holmes, he knew, had a poor opinion of his talents. He never felt quite at ease with Monckton and could not get on with Murray. He was scarcely on speaking terms with Townshend. He was obsessed by the fear of having to return to England without taking Quebec, and of being 'exposed to the censure of an ignorant populace'. It if came to that, he would quit the Service, which in any case he was 'determined to do', he told his mother despairingly, 'the first opportunity'. And yet there was not one of the senior officers with whom he felt he could discuss his problems. He had forced himself into a position of utter loneliness. He had even quarrelled recently with some of the officers on his normally submissive staff and in particular with Colonel Carleton, who in consequence was guilty of what the loyal Captain Bell referred to as 'abominable behaviour'. Plan after plan came into his restless mind and was rejected, or in a moment of enthusiasm accepted and then as suddenly thrown away. Several times during these long August days he decided on a plan of action, gave detailed orders for its implementation, and then a few hours later cancelled them all. 'Within the space of three hours', a staff officer complained, 'we received at the General's request three different orders of consequence, which were contradicted immediately after their reception; which indeed has been the constant practice of the General ever since we have been here, to the no small amazement of every one who has the liberty of thinking.' Perhaps it kept the men alert, perhaps it gave would-be deserters a false idea of his intentions, but it also could not help but give an impression of a strangely indecisive leadership. His orders, Murray plaintively commented when the campaign was over, showed 'little stability, stratagem or fixed intention'. It was an understandable verdict. In the Navy too, despite his reputation for recklessness, he was considered curiously hesitant and slow. He appeared to have lost his nerve. 'General Wolfe', Captain Schomberg confided to Admiral Forbes, 'appears more like Fulvius Maximus than Achilles; notwithstanding what is said of his impetuosity.'

As their leader wrestled anxiously and indeterminately with his problems the soldiers' health declined in the changeable August weather. The field hospitals were full of dysentery cases, and every morning scores of men woke up with aching, shivering limbs and feverish eyes. By the end of the month there were more than a thousand men sick and injured in the field hospitals. Millions of black, drearily buzzing flies fell down on the cook-houses and on the roofs of tents and in the latrines, like swarms of locusts. The days were generally sultry and hot, and in spite of the General Orders that the camps should be swept 'sweet and clean' and all offal and filth burned, the smell of them was often revolting. There was no straw, and the troops had to make do with spruce boughs or green corn, and to rip out the floor boards from farmhouses as duckboards for their tents. Rations too were running short, and the troops were reduced to eating horse-flesh, for all beef and mutton and the cattle brought in by the marauding detachments had to be sent to the hospitals. The prices of goods in the sutlers' tents were uncommonly high. Cheshire cheese was 10*d.* a pound, Bristol beer 1*s.* 6*d.* a bottle, lump sugar 1*s.* 6*d.* a pound and Hyson tea as much as 2*s.* an ounce. A pound of roll tobacco cost 1*s.* 10*d.* and a pound of hard soap 1*s.* Lemons varied between 3*s.* and 6*s.* a dozen. A soldier's pay of 5*s.* 10*d.* a week did not go very far with prices this high, particularly as he received it only at irregular intervals and then with 1*s.* 8*d.* a week deducted for wear and tear of clothing and with other deductions for Chelsea Hospital, grease and powder for his queue, and the fees of the Quartermaster-

General, the regimental surgeon, and the regimental agent.

But despite their prices the goods were readily sold, for there was nothing else for the troops to spend their money on when they got it and nowhere else for them to spend it. Occasionally a soldier, or a group of sailors or marines from the ships anchored in the river, would break regulations and wander off beyond the army's limits into the woods and fields in search of fresh vegetables or, even more hopelessly, a complaisant farm girl. But they never returned and later their scalped bodies were found by the side of forest tracks without muskets and with empty pockets.

The lack of fresh vegetables had led to many cases of scurvy in the army, as well as in the fleet, and it was a disease which the men took pains and risks to avoid. This was not so much because of its unpleasant effects as because it was not always considered necessary to send men to an easy life in the hospital compound for its treatment. A rougher and more traditional remedy was the earth bath, which involved the naked patient standing in a pit in the ground and being buried up to his neck in mould. He was left buried in his packing of mould with only his head showing above ground for several hours, like a Russian peasant woman convicted of murdering her husband. The operation was repeated every day until the patient was cured; or, as sometimes happened, contracted some other and more serious malady.

It was not only the men who were sickening. The General himself was obviously far from well. In the morning, when he came out of the cottage at Montmorency, the staff at his headquarters saw how pale and tired he looked. His bright red hair emphasized the pallor of his thin, neurotic face, while his deeply shadowed eyes and blotchy skin were the telling results of nights of worry and despair. He was curt and bad-tempered, snapping at his officers and berating the men. But sometimes he would make an effort to go out of his way to speak to a soldier or a young officer and then dismiss him with a kind and weary smile, and it was on these occasions that the soldiers, looking up into the ill, momentarily sympathetic face of their young General, felt, with pity, that they would die for him. It was a love of a sort, spontaneous and unquestioning.

Few of the senior officers had any such illusions. They had to work with him and live more closely with him than the junior officers and soldiers had to do. They had to bear the brunt of his ill-temper, put up with his moody silences, and keep pace with his tireless, restless mind. Ordinary conversation with him was impossible. He thought of nothing but Quebec. One day some of the officers on his staff were discussing a fellow-officer who had a poor constitution. 'Don't talk to me of constitution,' Wolfe snapped. 'If he has spirit, that's enough. Spirit will carry a man through anything.'

And however much they disliked the man personally, however much they criticized his handling of the operations, his officers could not but admit that the spirit which the General himself displayed was remarkable. Ill as he was, he went out every day whatever the weather to inspect a forward position, alter the siting of a gun, or with an aide crawl forward as close as he could get to the Montmorency cataract and peer ahead, lost in thought, for minutes on end. At the first sign of any French movements, the first sound of musket shots or a more intense bombardment, he rushed to the scene of activity to see if it was something he could turn to his advantage. The nervous energy of the man was limitless ; his personal courage astounding. He would not give in. He would not give in to his health and he would not give in to the seemingly unassailable Montcalm. The suggestion that he should leave a small fortified post on the Ile aux Coudres and sail away until the following spring was, after the briefest consideration, rejected. 'I'll have Quebec', he said, 'if I have to stay here until November.' And no one doubted that he meant it.

But on the morning of 19 August when the staff at the Montmorency headquarters were waiting for the punctual appearance of the General outside his cottage door, Captain Hervey Smith came out to announce that he was at last so sick he could not get out of bed. His illness had come to a crisis. The news spread like wildfire round the army. The General was dying. Wolfe, himself, believed that he might die. For years he had believed that he was near to death. 'A few years more or less are of little consequence to the common run of men', he had written to his mother with familiar solemnity some time before. 'And therefore I need not lament that I am perhaps somewhat nearer to my end than others of my time.' But to die in bed after a humiliating and costly failure was unthinkable. If he was to die it was a hero's death that he must have. A few days before he had been heard to say that he 'would cheerfully sacrifice a leg or an arm to be in possession of Quebec'. But now it was more than a limb that he must give. His surgeon afterwards remembered with what intensity the General begged him, with bright and feverish eyes, to make him well enough to get on to the field of battle. 'I know you cannot cure my complaint', he told him, 'but patch me up so that I may be able to do my duty for the next few days and I shall be content.'

As Wolfe's surgeon bled and drugged his patient in his endeavours to get him on his feet again, the activities of the army continued and the marauding parties went deeper and deeper into Canadian territory, burning and ravaging the timber houses and the well-tilled lands. But these irregular operations lowered the morale and the standard of discipline of an already softening army. The soldiers were no longer merely unwell, they were becoming unruly.

They had recently merited some Orders of particular

asperity, and punishments had been heavy. The day before he was confined to bed Wolfe had found it necessary to issue a General Order that 'if a soldier pretends to dispute the authority of an officer of another corps under whose command he is, and if any soldier presumes to use any indecent language to the N.C.O. of his unit or another corps, such soldier shall be punished in an exemplary manner'.

Insubordination was bad enough, but desertion was worse, and deserters were swimming across the river in twos and threes almost daily. 'Any soldier', the General ordered in an attempt to stem this growing trickle of desertion, 'who passes the out-sentries *on any pretence whatsoever* shall be brought to a court-martial and punished.' But the tempting sight of Quebec was too much for the more imaginative and less conscientious of the men. They imagined behind those imposing walls the well-equipped brothels and wine-cellars of a comfortably entrenched army ; and in spite of the storm of shells and cannon shot which rained constantly upon the town they felt the pull of it irresistibly. And then for some of them there was the chance perhaps of a new life in a vast and lovely country far away to the south. As for the army, all they seemed to do in his regiment nowadays, a corporal in the 60th petulantly complained, was to march up and down the river bank to muddle the French and to burn corn.

'The outposts and guards are to be more careful for the future', the General Orders warned on 25 August, 'in stopping all soldiers who are found attempting to slip by them.'

But the next day seven marines paddled across the river in a captured canoe, and a few days later eight soldiers of Otway's Regiment followed them on a raft. The trickle of desertion was becoming a stream.

The men were also beginning to lose their nerve. Night after night in their outposts they listened with dry mouths to the sounds of cracking twigs and the rustle of leaves in the undergrowth, holding their breath. This was a new and nerve-shattering kind of warfare, very different from the battles in the open with a seen and respected enemy which they had learned to expect and to understand. Here the enemy were all around you in the night, unseen and unheard, with tomahawks hanging from their naked thighs and with scalping knives between their painted lips. Sometimes a pair of sentries coming to relieve an outpost would hear no beckoning whisper from the trench, and then, crawling closer, their scalps tickling with apprehension and fear, they would see the crumpled bodies and the mutilated heads. Long nights at the edge of the woods had so broken the nerve of some units that the soldiers' fingers were always mentally on their musket triggers, ready to fire without orders or warning.

A private of the 47th Regiment who had escaped from captivity in an Indian village returned to his unit to tell a horrible story. He had struggled free from his bonds, he said, the night before he was to have provided the main course at a feast on the following day. For three days the villagers, women and children as well as men, had taken turns at torturing him. They had stuck splinters of wood behind his fingernails and up his penis, exploded little pockets of gunpowder which had been packed into cuts in his flesh made with the edge of a tomahawk blade, and smashed his toes to pulp with stone hammers. Young girls had pulled the hairs off his chest and little boys had poked sticks and brambles up his nose. The horrible details of his experiences were repeated and exaggerated until the very thought of an Indian was enough to send a shiver down the spine.

One day a working-party cutting fascines in the woods by the Montmorency River, under a small guard of light infantry, saw a small group of Indians stealthily approaching through the trees. With shouts of fear and horror the men rushed to their muskets and let off in every direction, killing and wounding each other in terrified panic. And on the same day a sergeant and fourteen men of the 48th Regiment killed several American rangers whom they mistook for Indians. On 22 August two sentries were ordered by their colonel to stand for an hour at the latrines with women's caps on their heads for screaming and firing in terror at an imaginary band of redskins. They were 'for the future to march in front of all parties without a grain of powder in their pieces'. Another man convicted of cowardice was made to ride a wooden horse, wearing a petticoat with a broom in his hand and a notice on his back saying 'This is the Reward of my Merit'. Some of the women of the Army jeered at him and threw sticks and lumps of earth in his face until a volunteer chased them away with a tomahawk.

But bad as things were with the British Army, the plight of the French did not seem much better. The beautiful town of Quebec was being slowly destroyed by the batteries at Pointe de Lévy. By the beginning of the month a French officer estimated that four thousand shells and nearly ten thousand cannon shot had already been fired at the town, and now the fire of the thirty-two-pounder guns at the batteries was being supplemented by thirteen-inch naval mortars with a range of nearly three miles. Fires were constantly breaking out in the Lower Town. In the Upper Town a hundred and sixty-seven houses were destroyed in a single terrible night. On 10 August a shell had crashed through into a cellar, ignited a vat of brandy and started a fire which had burned down many beautiful buildings, including Notre Dame des Victoires. That part of the town overlooking the river was in ruins.

Rations in the town and in the army were short and were becoming shorter. Supply ships were now frequently intercepted by Holmes's flotilla in the St Lawrence as they sailed up from Montreal and Trois Rivières, while the shortage of horses and pack animals made land transport a difficult alternative. A large convoy of provisions which got through to Quebec towards the end of the month was commandeered by Bigot, who saw to it that his friends got a grossly unfair share. The hungry French troops made up their rations by taking what their quartermasters could not give them from the farms and stores of the Canadians ; while the Canadian milita, seeing their countrymen robbed and pillaged by English and French alike and watching the crops ripening in the fields, now began to desert in large numbers. As the harvest got under way, towards the end of the month, as many as two hundred militiamen crept off in the night to return to their farms.

Murray's activities in the upper river were also causing the French command concern and had induced Montcalm to send Bougainville from Beauport with fifteen hundred men to strengthen the thin line of troops between Quebec and Cap Rouge and thus stretch out his already extended front for nearly twenty miles. Although Murray's first two attempts to gain a footing on the northern shore had failed and had cost him a hundred and forty men, the third assault which he had made on 19 August had been successful. He had got a large force ashore at Deschambault, and had set fire to a big warehouse containing 'all the effects, including equipage and apparel of all the officers in Quebec, civil and military, besides arms and ammunition'.

A greater worry to the French than Murray's raids, however, was the growing English fleet in that part of the river. Vaudreuil saw now the fundamental mistake he had made in sending the French frigates up river to Trois Rivières and keeping the crews to man the floating batteries and the guns in Quebec. On 10 August he made another attack on the British ships. The method used on this occasion was a 'fire-organ'—a boat containing several tubes filled with bits of jagged iron and tar lashed across a timber box—which was to be rowed towards the fleet. At the last moment, before the raiders jumped overboard, a slow-burning match was to be lit and the match in turn would ignite a train of gunpowder which would lead to the explosion of the craft just as it reached the English anchorage. Unfortunately, the nervous crew of the 'fire-organ' acted too soon, and, instead of burning several ships as intended, only five English sailors were injured as they towed the spluttering machine out of range to beach it on the northern shore.

Realizing that a more conventional attack would have to be made, Vaudreuil then ordered the French crews back to their ships at Trois Rivières for an attack upon Holmes's fleet. As soon as the sailors arrived the French frigates sailed downstream and on sighting the English ships formed up in as adequate a battle formation as the narrow channel and the difficulties of navigation would allow. But now it was too late. After a few shots laid across the English bows, fired more in protest than in hope of victory, the French commander, realizing how hopelessly outnumbered he was, thought it best not to risk his small flotilla in an action which it seemed impossible for him to win and so retired to anchor, sending the smaller ships up the St Lawrence tributaries and out of harm's way.

The French, nevertheless, considered all these to be minor setbacks. They were still confident of the final victory. Their position was after all just as impregnable now as it had ever been. Wolfe's guns might ultimately destroy Quebec, but his men could never take it.

At the beginning of the month there had seemed a possibility that the town might fall owing to French reverses in the south. Amherst had captured Ticonderoga and was advancing up the shores of Lake Champlain towards Montreal; while another army under John Prideaux had advanced westward from Albany along the Mohawk route towards Niagara, and although Prideaux had been killed by an exploding shell the fortress had been surrendered to his second-in-command, Sir William Johnson, five days later. Amherst's slow but sure advance on Montreal had made it necessary for Lévis, Montcalm's most experienced officer, to be sent from Quebec with fifteen hundred men to help in the organization of its defence.

But now more cheering despatches were received from the French south of Montreal. Amherst for some reason had stopped. Spies reported that he did not appear to be making any efforts to advance farther; and Bourlamaque, having retreated to Ile aux Noix, a naturally defensive position in the middle of the Richelieu River, wrote that he was confident of holding it, particularly as he had four heavily armed French ships under his command and Amherst had nothing with which to combat them.

Montcalm's worries about the army behind him were for the moment over. He released two thousand of his Canadian militiamen to go and help with the harvest. He could turn once more with his whole attention to look down across the wide river at the enemy below him.

'Two months more', he told an aide, 'and they will be gone.'

II

WOLFE was recovering. He was weak and excessively
pale but the fever had abated and by 22 August,
although not yet strong enough to get out of bed,
he was issuing orders, dictating letters, and making plans
with familiar industry.

Murray's slow return from the upper river, after repeated
orders to get his men back at once, infuriated him. For days
he had been sending messages through to him, and Murray
had apparently been ignoring them. 'Murray', he told
Monckton despairingly, 'by his long absence above and
by detaining all our boats, is actually master of the operations—or rather puts an entire stop to them.' And then on
29 August he was, at last, given news of Murray's return.

On the same day Monckton received from the General's
headquarters a letter which suggested that the three brigadiers should meet and so 'that the public service may not
suffer by the General's indisposition' they were asked to be
so 'good as to consult together for the public utility and
advantage, and consider of the best method of attacking the
enemy'.

'If the French Army is attacked and defeated', the letter
continued, 'the General concludes the town would immediately surrender, because he does not find they have any
provisions in the place.

'The General is of opinion the army should be attacked in
preference to the place, because of the difficulties of pene-
trating from the Lower to the Upper Town.

'There appear three methods of attacking the Army.'

Each of these methods was a variation on the same theme —an attack on the centre of the French line at Beauport— which seems never to have left Wolfe's mind since the terrible disaster there at the end of July. One plan was for a large detachment to ford the Montmorency and attack the French in the rear, while a secondary force simultaneously attacked from the front; another was for the light infantry and grenadiers to advance along the mud flats at the bottom of the cliff-face at low tide and then assault the upper entrenchments while the main force landed from the boats; the third plan was for all the troops to engage in a mass frontal assault on the Beauport shore at low water.

Monckton called a meeting of his fellow-brigadiers to consider these suggestions the day after he received them. Townshend and Murray took no trouble to conceal their opinion that all three plans recommended by the General were both foolhardy and unimaginative. Any plan of attack was dangerous, but why choose to attack the enemy on ground which was not only a natural line of defence but which was also heavily defended? Why select a spot where an attack had already ignominiously failed and from which the enemy could fall back to a second line of defence along the St Charles River? Why not attack him in a place which was admittedly as difficult to reach, but which, if once taken, would cut him off from his supplies? If one last desperate attempt to take Quebec were to be made before the winter ice closed the river, the place to attack was the north shore above the town. They were all agreed about this. And they began to formulate a detailed plan and to draft a reply to the General's letter.

They decided to suggest that the artillery and infantry should be moved from Montmorency to Ile d'Orléans, which should be put into a good state of defence with six hundred men; six hundred men should also be left to defend Pointe de Lévy while the remainder of the army should encamp with two months' provisions on the west side of the

Echemin River above the town; the attack should be made at night somewhere near Cap Rouge.

'The natural strength of the enemy's situation', they wrote in explanation of their outright rejection of Wolfe's suggestions, 'between the rivers St Charles and Montmorency, now improved by all the art of their engineers, makes the defeat of the enemy, if attacked there, very doubtful.' The suggestion of fording the Montmorency River and attacking the French rear was in their opinion 'exposed to certain discovery and consequently to the disadvantage of a constant wood fight'. If the army did manage to gain a footing on the Beauport shore Montcalm could still defend the St Charles River while Quebec was reinforced.

On the other hand, a successful assault above the town would enable them to get between Quebec and its line of supply, and the French would be forced to fight or to starve. 'If we can establish ourselves on the north shore', they insisted, 'the Marquis de Montcalm must fight us on our own terms.'

Before sending this letter to Wolfe, Monckton took a copy to Saunders and to Holmes. Both admirals approved it, and in the face of such complete agreement Wolfe accepted it. At the end of a long despatch to Pitt which he was at this time finishing, he told him of his decision.

I found myself so ill, and am still so weak, [he wrote] that I begged the General officers to consult together for the general utility. They are all of opinion that as more ships and provisions are now got above the town, they should try, by conveying up a corps of four or five thousand men (which is nearly the whole strength of the Army after the Points of Levi and Orleans are left in a proper state of defence), to draw the enemy from their present situation and bring them to an action. I have acquiesced in the proposal; and we are preparing to put it into execution. . . .

To the uncommon strength of the country the enemy have added, for the defence of the river, a great number of floating batteries and boats: by the vigilance of these, and the Indians round

116

our different posts, it has been impossible to execute anything by surprise. . . . By the list of disabled officers . . . you may perceive that the army is much weakened. . . .

In this situation there is such a choice of difficulties that I own myself at a loss how to determine. The affairs of Great Britain, I know, require the most rigorous measures; but then the courage of a handful of brave men should be exerted, only when there is some hope of a favourable event. However you may be assured, Sir, that the small part of the campaign which remains shall be employed (as far as I am able) for the honour of his Majesty and the interest of the nation.

Now that the army officers had at last decided on a definite plan of action Admiral Saunders was determined to do all he could to see that they carried it out without delay. He had constantly warned them of the dangers of leaving the operations until too late in the season. In a few weeks' time, whatever happened, he would have to get his ships out of the river and into the open sea, otherwise they would never reach it. Holmes's flotilla above the town was now composed of more than twenty vessels, and he was ready to carry out any orders which might be given him. At Saunders' insistence, a meeting was held in Wolfe's cottage on the evening of 31 August, and that night the plans for the evacuation of the camp at Montmorency were made. Earlier in the day, to the amazement of the entire staff, Wolfe sent sixteen hundred men away on detachment 'to lay waste such parishes as shall presume to persist in their opposition'. In view of the already depleted numbers available for the forthcoming attack his action was considered 'entirely inexplicable'. It remains so still.

The evacuation of the Montmorency camp was carried out on 3 September. And although simple enough compared with what was to follow, it came close to disaster. Orders had been given for the burning of a barn in front of Townshend's headquarters and for the use of other fires as signals to the various units giving them notice of when it was time to file down to the boats at the river's edge. But the fires got out of hand. It was impossible to distinguish one signal from another, and the fires not only muddled the officers but gave Montcalm clear warning of their intentions. Believing that at last he had an opportunity of striking a blow at Wolfe without risk to himself, he crossed the Montmorency ford with a large force and prepared to attack the disorganized brigades as they stumbled off towards the embarkation points. The situation was saved by Monckton, who by the light of flares noisily embarked two battalions in landing-craft to make a feint at the Beauport shore. Montcalm, true to his fixed policy of taking no chances, brought his men back again across the river, and the evacuation of the British camp to Ile d'Orléans was completed, in hopeless disorder but without further danger.

The following morning the whole army, both on Ile d'Orléans and at Pointe de Lévy, was drawn up on parade, and Wolfe inspected his men. Of the eight thousand, five hundred troops who had left Louisbourg in June there were now scarcely more than half still fit for duty. The hospitals were full of sick and wounded, and many of the best men were dead.

Wolfe looked ill and distracted. When asked by an ingenuous officer on his staff if calling out the entire army like this meant that there was some important operation afoot, he turned away and would not answer him. That ·evening he dined with Monckton and the officers of the Brigadier's staff, but when he returned to his tent Barré saw that he was 'deadly ill'. Once more the surgeon was summoned urgently and Wolfe begged him to patch him up again. He was feverish and on the verge of mental collapse. The disease of his bladder seemed to be reaching a painful climax. All next day he lay sweating on his bed, breathing convulsively and in terrible pain. Towards evening, after letting pints of blood and administering various medicines, the surgeon had managed to bring down his temperature and ease the pain. In the morning, his eyes glittering unnaturally in his paper-white face, he was on his feet again.

He was determined that it should not be left to his brigadiers to make the final arrangements, and particularly not to choose the actual landing-place. With death or glory now in sight he dragged himself from bed in his passionate fear that he was not fulfilling his duty, that he was being left out of the limelight. He must himself lead his men to victory or he must be killed.

From that morning onwards he consulted no one, asked for no advice and no opinion. He kept his own counsel to the point of secretiveness, sometimes giving a junior officer important information which he would deny to his brigadiers. Having told Pitt that the general scheme of attack was the brigadiers' idea and not his own, he would not perhaps be held entirely responsible if it failed. But if it succeeded he must at all costs share in the acclaim. 'Every step he takes is wholly his own,' an officer commented; 'I'm told he asks no one's opinion, and wants no advice.'

Townshend's irritation and misery were pathetic. His letters to Charlotte, his 'most dear wife', provide eloquent testimony as to his state of mind. The sight of the captive women and children, he told her, made him feel miserable and dejected and long for home. He thought of his wife and children constantly, and the letters from his little four-year-old son George always brought tears to his eyes.

I never served so disagreeable a campaign as this, [he complained in one letter.] Our unequal force has reduced our Operations to a scene of Skirmishing, Cruelty and Devastation. It is War of the worst Shape. A Scene I ought not to be in. For the future believe me, my dear Charlotte, I will seek the reverse of it. . . . General Wolf's [sic] health is but very bad. His generalship, in my poor opinion, is not a bit better. He never consulted any of us till the latter end of August, so that we have nothing to answer for, I hope, as to the success of the campaign.

119

On 6 September Wolfe himself superintended the sudden, alarming bombardments from the batteries, designed to keep the enemy in uncertainty as to his real intentions. He organized, without reference to the brigadiers, the complicated marching and embarking orders of the main body of troops who could be seen by the French filing hour after hour along the south bank of the river from Pointe de Lévy to the Echemin River, through which they waded up to their thighs in the cold water towards the waiting boats, stumbling as they tried to stand upright and maintain their balance on the slippery bed beneath the rapid currents. They held their muskets above the water, ignoring, in their anxiety not to fall under, plops and showers of spray made by the shots of the French snipers from the opposite bank.

Wolfe worked all day and most of the night, stopping with obvious impatience and reluctance to eat a hurried meal or to get a few hours' sleep, kept alive by the force of his burning will to triumph.

By the evening of 6 September Wolfe had got three thousand, six hundred men aboard Holmes's flotilla and he was ready to sail. A further twelve hundred men under Colonel Burton remained on Pointe de Lévy to act as reinforcements if the main assault were successful.

The following morning was sunny and warm, and a gentle breeze had come up. The French soldiers along the river line watched as the boats sailed gently upstream, their decks packed with the red coats of the English soldiers, their flags and pennants proudly streaming against the blue, unclouded sky. The flotilla sailed unmolested as far as Cap Rouge, where Bougainville was now entrenched with three thousand men. At sight of the approaching boats the Canadians under Bougainville's command rushed down from the cliff-top, shouting and cheering, to man the batteries at the water's edge. The British soldiers could see quite clearly the blue and grey uniforms of the Canadians and the few white uniforms of the French regulars milling about excitedly behind the earthworks.

In the afternoon Holmes's ships opened fire as the sailors rowed up and down opposite the French defences as if looking for a possible landing-place.

Meanwhile Wolfe himself was peering through his telescope at the northern shore, also looking for a place to land. All day long he had been leaning against the rail of a sloop slowly sailing upstream as far as Pointe aux Trembles. It has been suggested that he was accompanied on this trip as on earlier ones by Major Robert Stobo, who had arrived from Halifax a few days previously. Stobo had been sent as a prisoner to Quebec after Washington's defeat at Fort Necessity and had escaped from the town in company with an American ranger named Stevens. He was certainly thoroughly familiar with the ground on the French side of the river, and it is unlikely that Wolfe would not have called on him for his local knowledge. In the evening, as soon as the reconnaissance was over, he was sent by Wolfe on a dangerous mission through the French lines to carry despatches to Amherst.

The place decided upon for the landing was a small concavity in the cliff a little way below Pointe aux Trembles. It was several miles from Quebec, and it might be possible for the army to gain a footing here before the French realized what was happening, and then by advancing on Bougainville at Cap Rouge to draw the French into battle on the plains before Quebec. Wolfe's decision was not communicated to his brigadiers, but they were given some indication of where the landing was intended and instructed to make their own reconnaissance in the area. While they were doing so on 9 September Wolfe decided against his original plan and 'found out another place more to his mind'. Again it is not definitely known what induced the General once more to cancel his instructions. Townshend, without further comment, laconically reported that 'by some intelligence the General had, he has changed his mind as to the place he intended to land'. It seems possible that the intelligence came from the Rev. Michael Houdin, a French priest who had renounced the Roman Catholic faith and had become an Anglican missionary to the Mohawks. Like Stobo, Houdin knew Quebec and its environs well, and throughout the siege acted as chaplain to the 48th Regiment and as an intelligence officer at Wolfe's headquarters. He had, perhaps, learned from deserters that a detachment of Canadian troops, weak in numbers and morale, was defending a cleft in the cliff-face a mile and a half above Quebec known as the Anse au Foulon. Commanding this detachment was a Captain de Vergor, a Canadian officer of exceptional inadequacy who had been tried for cowardice after the surrender at Beauséjour and had only been saved by the intervention of Bigot, a gambling crony. Winding up the cliff at this point was a zigzag path, broken here and there by felled trees and barricades. It was steep and slippery, but it did seem that it might be possible to clamber up it. Everywhere between Quebec and Cap Rouge the sharp ascent would be difficult, and the Anse au Foulon seemed no more difficult than anywhere else. At the top there was a cluster of tents, but so far as could be determined from the southern bank there were only about twelve of them and few white uniforms had ever been seen in the small encampment. This, Wolfe decided, would be the place, and he asked his aide-de-camp to warn the senior officers that they would be required to accompany him on a survey the next morning.

A particular advantage in landing at the Anse au Foulon was that the chances of surprising the enemy might be much greater at this point than higher upstream near Pointe aux Trembles, where the attack was more likely to be expected. The element of surprise might be further increased by the army sailing up river the night before the attack as if an assault were intended several miles above the town and then drifting back unseen on the ebb tide to land quite close to it.

These thoughts must have occurred to Wolfe in making his choice of the Anse au Foulon as the landing-place, but so much was later to work in his favour because of this decision that the possibility of French treachery cannot be ignored. It is certain that Bigot and Cadet, and indeed most officials in Quebec, were looking for a French defeat as the only hope of covering up their years of swindling, which at last were being suspected in Paris. They may then have ensured that Wolfe got the information that a landing at the Anse au Foulon would be only half-heartedly resisted. The subsequent troop movements in the area and the suspicious mistakes made there can certainly be explained on this assumption.

The first clue is afforded by the appointment of the incompetent Vergor to command the detachment on the cliff-top. For the appointment was a very recent one. Until a day or two previously the troops here had been commanded by Captain St Martin, a French regular officer, specially chosen for the duty by Montcalm. St Martin, despite repeated blandishments, had refused the Canadians under his command permission to go on leave to their homes to help with the harvest. Vergor on the other hand granted leave to any man who wanted to return to his farm on condition that when his harvest had been gathered in he agreed to put in several hours' work on Vergor's farm. The numbers of men at the Anse au Foulon at the critical time had thus dwindled to a mere token force as small as it was unwary.

Montcalm's orders were not only countermanded in respect of the appointment of the officer to command this important detachment. This on its own might not have proved disastrous. More serious for the French command were the mysterious movements of the Guienne Regiment.

This regiment had been ordered by Montcalm to take up position on the plains outside Quebec, between the town walls and the Anse au Foulon. It was a crack regiment with a reliable colonel, and Montcalm believed that it could safely be relied upon to delay the advance of the British on Quebec should they attempt a landing that side of the town. Vaudreuil, without reference to the Commander-in-Chief and no doubt on the suggestion of Bigot and Cadet, who were constantly in his company, now ordered the withdrawal of the regiment to the line of the River St Charles. The plains to the west of Quebec were thus left virtually undefended.

And later on they were also to be less well patrolled. For on the very night before the attack Captain de Remigny, an extremely intelligent officer in command of the most active and observant river post between Cap Rouge and the Anse au Foulon, lost his three horses. One was stolen and the other two were lamed.

But how much of all this, if any of it, came about through French treachery may never now be known. Wolfe destroyed the September entries in his diary, and if he told any members of his staff that his decision was based on something more than intelligence reports and tactical considerations, none of them afterwards reported this. It is certain that he told his brigadiers and the admirals nothing. And when they received the message that the plan of attack had been altered they were all surprised and most of them were exasperated.

As Townshend had all day been considering the possibility and problems of an assault at Pointe aux Trembles, his ill-tempered reaction to the aide-de-camp's message was understandable. Admiral Holmes also showed his irritation. 'The alteration of the plan of operations', he reported, 'was not, I believe, approved of by many besides himself. It had been proposed to him a month before, when the first ships passed the town, and when it was entirely defenceless and unguarded. . . . He now laid hold of it when it was highly improbable he should succeed.'

It was accordingly a somewhat sulky and ill-humoured party which met on the morning of 10 September to carry out a survey of the cliff-face between Quebec and Sillery. The area to be covered by the reconnaissance was wide, as even now Wolfe did not care to reveal the exact place he had decided on to any of the officers who were to accompany him.

Brigadiers Monckton and Townshend, Admiral Holmes, Colonel Carleton, Major Mackellar (now recovered from a severe wound he had received during the attack on the Beauport coast), and Captain Delaune, a gallant officer who was to have an important part in the assault, silently followed Wolfe into the boats under an escort of thirty men from the 43rd Regiment. They were all, except Holmes, dressed in grenadiers' overcoats to deceive the French look-outs, but as they did not trouble to do up the buttons their disguise was quite ineffective. A French officer at Sillery who saw them through his glass reported to Bougainville the presence in the river of 'three boats of the enemy, carrying many officers in gay uniforms, one in particular in a blue surtout with much gold lace'.

Meanwhile scores of landing-craft packed with grey-faced, grumbling soldiers drifted down river with the ebb tide, merely to return with the flood. This constant, tiresome oscillation had been going on for days and was as exhausting for the men who were compelled to sit, cramped and seasick, in the rolling boats as for the French and Canadians on the cliff-top above them who marched and countermarched, following them up and down, day and night, like shadows.

The day before, the grim and boring peripatetic had been broken when the weather was so bad and the river so rough that the men became weak with seasickness and their officers feared that if they were kept much longer in the boats they would be too feeble to reach the tops of the cliffs when they got out of them. About half of the men, therefore, were put ashore in the village of St Nicholas, where they slept off the effects of their illness in the group of buildings round the church and in the church itself. That evening, however, the strong easterly wind shifted, the skies cleared, and most of the men, a few of them still shivering and reeking of vomit, had been put back once more into the crowded boats.

The drifting of the landing-craft and the corresponding forced marches along the cliffs continued.

On 10 September Saunders summoned the other naval commanders aboard his flagship. He told them that he thought the time had come to tell the land officers that the fleet could no longer remain in the river. Holmes and the others agreed. The short summer season of navigation was almost over. Under the admiral's care were more than thirteen thousand men, almost a quarter of the strength of the entire British Navy, and it would be absurd to run the risk of their being frozen up in the St Lawrence for the winter. Already the floes of soft, thin ice would be forming in the Gulf and at the mouth of the river. Wolfe must be informed that the lateness of the season required the immediate withdrawal of the fleet.

On receipt of the Admiral's notification Wolfe rushed to the flagship. He told Saunders that he could not believe the Navy would jeopardize the whole campaign for the sake of a few more days. He had now found a good place for scaling the cliff. He intended to send up one hundred and fifty picked men to 'feel the way', and if they gained a footing at the top the others would follow ; the French would be forced to fight and, win or lose, the campaign would be over. If his chosen men could not get to the top, why then, no one could, and he would withdraw the rest and go home.

Admiral Saunders, whose threat to sail away was perhaps made only to force the army into immediate action, agreed without hesitation. The army could rely on him for his most active co-operation. His only concern was that Quebec should be taken soon and that he should get his ships away down river before the ice packs shut them in. He was, he told Wolfe, ready and waiting for instructions, and so was Admiral Holmes. Indeed, it was already four days since the last ship detached for service under Holmes's command above the town had sailed into the upper river.

The ship was the smallest schooner in the fleet, and the proud way it sailed past the raging batteries in Quebec was an inspiration to all who saw it. Displacing only seventy tons and carrying less than thirty troops, she was named with touching disrespect *The Terror of France*. She sailed in broad daylight and in a gentle breeze under the roaring guns, her colours flying in calm defiance. On approaching the Admiral's flagship she gave a proud salute with her swivel guns as the sailors in the other ships cheered her to the echo.

Before leaving Saunders, Wolfe told him the details of his plan and asked him, when the day of the attack came, to create a diversion in the basin of Quebec by organizing a scene of great activity there. He was to put out lines of marking buoys and coloured flags, to get as many soldiers, sailors, and marines as he could into landing-craft and then when the real attack had started and a prearranged signal had been given he was to open up with all his guns on the Beauport shore and thus lead Montcalm to suppose that the real attack was intended there. All the troops who could be collected from the hospitals on Ile d'Orléans, and spared from the batteries on Pointe de Lévy, would be available to him for this purpose.

If Saunders was satisfied that he had been told all he needed to know, the brigadiers were certainly not. Murray, who had been growing increasingly impatient with Wolfe's difficult attitude, had been further annoyed on 8 September when his orders to arrange with Monckton a pretended attack on the north shore at night with fifteen hundred men had been countermanded at the last minute owing to rough weather. And now, the very day before the attack in which the whole army was to be engaged, neither he nor either of the other two brigadiers had been told which was the selected landing-place. Monckton on 11 September had accompanied Wolfe on a reconnaissance to Goreham's Post, but the General had not been explicit. The brigadiers felt obliged to send a letter to ask for more precise information, previous verbal requests having been shrugged off. The correspondence was acrimonious.

> Sir [they wrote]. As we do not think ourselves sufficiently informed of the several parts which may fall to our share in the execution of the Descent which you intend to-morrow, we must beg leave to request from you as distinct orders as the nature of the thing will permit of, particularly as to the place and places we are to attack. This circumstance (perhaps very decisive) we cannot learn from the public orders, neither may it be in the power of the naval officer who leads the troops to instruct us. As we should be very sorry, no less for the public than our own sakes, to commit any mistakes, we are persuaded you will see the necessity of this application, which can proceed from nothing but a desire to execute your orders with the utmost punctuality.

The letter was signed by all three of them. At half past eight in the evening Wolfe wrote his reply aboard the *Sutherland*. He addressed it to Monckton.

> My reason for desiring the honour of your company with me to Goreham's Post yesterday was to shew you, as well as the distance would permit, the situation of the enemy, and the place where I meant they should be attacked; as you are charged with that duty I should be glad to give you all further light and assistance in my power—The place is called the *Foulon* distant upon two miles or two and a half from Quebec, where you remember an encampment of 12 to 13 tents and an abbatis below it.—You mentioned to-day that you had perceived a breastwork there, which made me imagine you as well acquainted with the place as the nature of things will admit of. I took Capt. Shads [*sic*] with me also and desired the

Admiral's attendance, that as the former is charged by Mr. Saunders with conducting of the boats, he might make himself as much a master of his post as possible; and as several of the Ships of War are to fall down with troops Mr Holmes would be able to station them properly after he had seen the place. . . . The officers who are appointed to conduct the divisions of boats have been strictly enjoined to keep as much order and to act as silently as the nature of the service will admit of, and Capt. Shads will begin to land the men a little of this side of the naked rock, which you must remember to have seen. . . . It is not usual [he added in a tone of petulance] to point out in the public orders the direct spot of our attack, nor for any inferior Officers not charged with a particular duty to ask instruction upon that point. I had the honour to inform you to-day that it is my duty to attack the French Army. To the best of my knowledge and abilities I have fixed upon that spot where we can act with the most force and are most likely to succeed. If I am mistaken, I am sorry and must be answerable to His Majesty and the public for the consequences.

Townshend was sent a separate letter, short and cold:

Brigadier-General Monckton is charged with the first landing and attack at the Foulon, if he succeeds you will be pleased to give directions that the troops afloat be set on shore with the utmost expedition, as they are under your command, and when 3,600 men now in the fleet are landed I have no manner of doubt but that we are able to fight and to beat the French Army, in which I know you will give your best assistance.

I have the honour to be, Sir,
Your most obedient and most humble servant.
JAM. WOLFE.

Murray, who was under Monckton's command, was ignored.

As Colonel Burton, commanding the troops (mainly of the 48th Regiment) left on Pointe de Lévy, had two days before received a long letter giving the General's intentions in some detail, the indignation of the brigadiers might well be considered justified.

129

Already that evening a group of staff officers on a last reconnaissance had been given evidence of Wolfe's touchy and irritable mood. Several versions of the incident have been recorded. The most likely one suggests that on their way back to the *Sutherland* the General had recited to his officers some verses from Gray's 'Elegy' which he had recently committed to memory and a copy of which, heavily annotated with platitudes, was afterwards found among his possessions. John Robison, the young tutor to an admiral's son, was in the boat and remembered thinking that the recitation could not have been 'so well received as he had expected, for the General suddenly broke off and said with a good deal of animation, "I can only say, Gentlemen, that if the choice were mine, I would rather be the author of these verses than win the battle which we are to fight to-morrow morning." ' After this abrupt protestation the remainder of the voyage was passed in embarrassed silence.

But Wolfe was in no mood to worry about the embarrassment of the officers on his staff or the resentment of his brigadiers. Indeed, he is reported to have said that evening that the brigadiers, all three of them, were unworthy of their commands. Two of them were cowards, and the third a villain. He was excited and restless, impatient for the operations to begin. Three days earlier he had reported to the Earl of Holdernesse, Secretary of State in Pitt's Government, that his 'constitution was entirely ruined', but what did that matter now if he were to win a great victory to-morrow and perhaps to die in doing it?

A few hours previously he had been given some information of extreme importance and great good fortune. Two deserters from Bougainville's camp had reported that provision-boats were to be sent down river on the ebb tide that night. It might well be possible, if he slipped downstream in front of the French, to mislead the sentries into believing that his boats were theirs. As it happened, the caulking of the store-ships was not completed that evening, so no French boats left Cap Rouge, but the sentries were not told and they were expecting them. Once again Wolfe was either extremely lucky or being helped by French treachery.

Everything was ready now. The General had issued his final orders. The men had been told that 'as there will be a necessity for remaining some part of the night in the boats, the officers will provide accordingly ; and the soldiers will have a gill of rum extraordinary to mix with their water ; arms and ammunition, two days provisions with rum and water, are all that the soldiers are to take into the boats. . . . The men to be quite silent and when they are about to land must not on any account fire out of the boats.' They were reminded that a 'vigorous blow struck by the army at this juncture may determine the fate of Canada. . . . The officers and men will remember what their country expects from them.' The watchword was to be 'Coventry'.

The remaining troops from St Nicholas had been embarked. The volunteers for the assault party had been selected. And the selection had been made in a familiar military way. Colonel Howe and Captain Delaune had asked for volunteers, promising that the names of those who survived would afterwards be recommended to the General for promotion. Only eight men had come forward, so these eight had been told to choose two other 'volunteers' each, to accompany them. But the twenty-four men eventually collected seemed a brave and trustworthy lot.

The complicated and crucially important business of organizing the timing of the operation and the movements of the landing-craft had been left in the capable hands of Captain Chads of the Navy, and that was something at least which Wolfe did not have to think about.

He tried to rest. There was nothing to do now but to wait.

On the cliffs above him Montcalm was waiting too.

Although he doubted now that the enemy would attack this season, he was as alert and prepared as he had always been. The day before he had written to Bourlamaque and told him that the enemy would certainly stay no longer than another month at the most. But he was ready for him should he decide to make a last assault before retiring for the winter. Every day he received reports from the French officer in command of a party of fifty Indians who paddled up and down the river watching the enemy's movements. He never for a moment relaxed his careful watchfulness. On 2 September he had written, 'The night is dark; it is raining; our troops are in their tents, dressed, ready for an alarm. I am in my boots; my horses are saddled. In fact this is my usual way. . . . I have not taken off my clothes since 23 June.'

Bougainville, who had been at Cap Rouge ever since Murray's raid on Deschambault, now had more than three thousand troops under his command. And his instructions were to watch the English all the time and wherever they went. 'M. Wolfe', Montcalm warned him, 'is just the man to double back in the night.' And he followed his instructions with painstaking care. He was a twenty-nine-year-old officer of exceptional intelligence. As Secretary at the French Embassy in London some years before he had been admitted to the Royal Society after having published an extremely learned work on integral calculus. He was as thorough and cautious as he was clever and he watched the river line as far upsteam as Jacques-Cartier with careful attention and followed the British boats whenever they moved from anchor. That night, however, there is reason to suppose that he was not at his headquarters but at Jacques-Cartier, nine miles farther from Quebec.

The evening before, Madame de Vienne, the wife of one of Bigot's subordinates whose house outside Quebec Vaudreuil was using as his headquarters, was advised to leave for Montreal. She was an attractive woman whose favours were apparently as much in demand as they were freely given. Although transport vehicles were in very short supply she had no difficulty in arranging for several pack animals and carts to be made available for her large quantities of luggage.

Bougainville heard of her departure on the evening of 11 September and immediately wrote to de Blau, an officer under his command at Jacques-Cartier, instructing him to keep the desirable Madame de Vienne there when she arrived. On 12 September de Blau replied that *'les dames n'ont point besoin de recommendations auprez de moi et Madame de Vienne moins qu'un autre'*.

Although there is no evidence to show that Bougainville spent the night with Madame de Vienne at Jacques-Cartier and not at his headquarters, his disastrous slowness in reaching the field of battle the following morning is otherwise difficult to explain.

In any case Bougainville might well have persuaded himself of the desirability of a visit to Jacques-Cartier; for most French officers, Montcalm included, felt that if an attack were to be made above Quebec it was more likely to be made here than nearer the town, where the steepness of the cliffs made an assault unlikely. 'We need not suppose', Montcalm said, 'that the enemy have wings.' 'A hundred men posted here', it was firmly believed, 'could stop their whole army.' It was a reasonable and justified view, and one which Vaudreuil certainly shared. He indeed seems to have believed that the persistent troop movements in the river were indications of withdrawal. 'Everything', he assured Bourlamaque, 'proves that the grand designs of the English have failed.'

12

IN the cramped cabin of the *Sutherland* Wolfe was
writing letters.

Around the ship in the dark and silent boats the
soldiers were whispering and waiting.

At nine o'clock on 13 September, 1759, Colonel Burton
on Pointe de Lévy collected together the twelve hundred
men under his command and embarked them in the flat-
bottomed boats waiting for them off Pointe aux Pères.
They left their tents standing so that the enemy should not
suspect that the camp had been deserted. The soldiers
climbed into the boats, quietly, without talking. In less than
an hour the boats were drifting up towards the main army.
They were disembarked on the southern shore, almost
opposite the Anse au Foulon, and waited there for the
landing-craft to pick them up after the assault on the
northern shore had been effected.

The weather was perfect. The night was dark, the moon
was not up, a soft but unrevealing light came from the stars.
Those ships of the main fleet which were still east of the
Echemin River now slipped anchor and sailed silently a
little way upstream, close to the southern shore against the
blackness of the bank, so that the French, should they see
them, might think that an attack was intended higher up.
But if the sentries did see them they took no notice, for boats
had been drifting up and down stream for days and nights
now, and they were tired of counting them. And so by
eleven o'clock the whole of Holmes's flotilla, and all the
flat-bottomed boats and landing-craft, were anchored undisturbed about six miles above the Anse au Foulon as
close to the southern shore as they could get, waiting in the

quiet darkness for the tide to turn. Soon after midnight the troops still on board the ships dropped overboard into the landing-craft.

At two o'clock in the morning the waters began to ebb. A lantern, its light shrouded from the northern shore, was hoisted up to the main topgallant mast-head of the *Sutherland*. It was the signal to cast off. Immediately the boats of the assaulting party slipped away downstream close to the southern shore. There was a slight breeze from the west and the ebb tide was running at three knots. Only occasionally did the sailors have to dip their oars into the water. After drifting silently for 'half a mile the boats changed course towards the northern shore. Half-way across the channel the leading boats came within sight of the sloop *Hunter*, anchored with shaded lights in midstream. Captain Smith, the master, who was on deck, gave orders for his guns to be trained on the oncoming craft in case they were French store-ships, but a soft call from the darkness reassured him and they passed by without mishap.

Close behind them followed the boats carrying the second wave of troops. Half an hour later the armed sloops slipped their anchors and they too were soon drifting downstream. By three o'clock the reserves and artillery under Townshend and the remaining transports and frigates were on the move and then the whole long line of boats drew slowly closer to the Anse au Foulon.

For a quarter of an hour the long armada glided quietly downstream, unchallenged and ignored, although the tide was flowing faster now and the boats were running dangerously close to the northern shore. And then suddenly the silence was broken by a shout from the river's edge on their left.

'*Qui vive?*'

For a moment no one spoke. The ripples lapped against the sides of the boats. The soldiers held their breath, tightly gripping their muskets. Then Simon Fraser, a young officer in the 78th Highlanders and son of their colonel, stood up in one of the leading boats and called in reply:

'*France! Et vive le Roi!*'

'*A quel régiment?*' the sentry called back.

'*De la Reine.*' Fraser believed it to be one of Bougainville's; but it had been detached from his command some time previously. Fortunately the sentry seemed to be unaware of this.

'*Pourquoi est-ce que vous ne parlez pas plus haut?*'

'*Tais-toi! Nous serons entendus.*'

The sentry was satisfied. The boats drifted past the post and the soldiers relaxed. One of them, an officer afterwards remembered with annoyance, giggled loudly in relief.

A few minutes later they rounded the heights of Samos, and the soldiers in the leading boats could see dimly in the darkness ahead the elbow of land, behind which was the Anse au Foulon. They did not have far to go now.

Again the silence was broken by a shout of challenge. Another sentry slithering down the cliff-face had rushed to the water's edge and shouted for the password.

This time Captain Donald MacDonald, also of the 78th Highlanders, replied.

'Provision-boats!' he called, the angry hoarse whisper disguising his accent. 'Don't make such a bloody noise. The —— English will hear us!'

The sentry waved them on. They could see the grey cuff of his uniform quite clearly against the black cliff.

They were round the headland now and the Anse au Foulon lay just ahead. The current was strong here and the boats were running fast with the tide. The sailors on a sudden order pushed out their oars and pulled hard against the rush of water, but they were drifting too fast and the boats were swept past the landing-place and came ashore some way farther downstream than Wolfe had intended.

It was too late to alter that now. Captain Delaune, Fraser, and MacDonald leapt out, followed by the other volunteers, and they all rushed with quiet determination at the cliff-face.

Wolfe with Barré and Hervey Smith jumped out soon after them and looked despairingly at the steep cliff. 'I don't think we can by any possible means get up here', Wolfe murmured, 'but we must use our best endeavour.' They stood on the shore listening anxiously for the sound of musket shots. It was a little after four o'clock.

Still there was silence. Although the cliff-face was steep there were more trees here than at the place which Wolfe had chosen, and perhaps they would manage to clamber up all right. They waited, straining their eyes and ears in the darkness. For minutes after the sounds of the volunteers had died away they could hear nothing but the rushing noise of the river, the rumble of gunfire from Pointe aux Pères, and the lapping, rippling waters of a stream which ran down the cliff at this point and gurgled over the rocks.

MacDonald and Delaune, leading the volunteers up the cliff, were the first to reach the top. As MacDonald advanced stealthily towards the group of tents he was challenged out of the darkness by a sentry. Again he replied in that hôarse and angry whisper. He'd been sent to relieve the post, he said; and he told the sentry to go back to the guard and tell the duty officer to call off all the other men along the cliff-top. 'I'll take care to give a good account of the —— English if they try to land.'

The sentry hesitated for a moment, unsure of what to do. By this time all twenty-four of the volunteers had reached the cliff-top and the silence was finally shattered. No one was sure who fired the first shot, but within seconds Vergor's camp was alive with the flashes of musket barrels and the shouts of terrified soldiers. Captain Vergor himself dashed out of his tent in his nightshirt, holding one hand in the air and firing his pistol wildly with the other. Then he ran away as fast as his bare feet would carry him, but he was shot in the ankle and fell screaming to the ground. The rest of his soldiers followed his example and fled. One or two were captured, but the rest got away.

Wolfe and the others waiting at the river's edge heard the musket shots and listened with fearful anxiety for the shouts of triumph. And now they came.

The General ordered the second wave of troops out of the boats and told them to get up the cliff as best they could. Some of the boats had drifted even farther downstream, and the men were already jumping out and trying to climb up the cliff in the face of a heavy fire from a few of Vergor's men who had been rallied there by a determined Canadian corporal. Wolfe leapt back into his boat and told the sailors to row him to within shouting distance of these men, whom he recalled to the Anse au Foulon. Then the sailors strained at their oars to get him back to the landing-place.

Bounding out of the boat when he reached it, he threw himself at the cliff and clambered up with a determination which was close to frenzy. His diseased body, weakened after days of blood-letting and feverish illness, was dragged up from tree to tree and from ledge to ledge by muscles forced to strain themselves once more, and perhaps now for the last time. All around him the surface of the cliff-face was crawling with stumbling, cursing soldiers. Over on his left a gang was working to remove the barricades and abattis on the zigzag path to make it easier for the men behind them. There was no need for silence now. The batteries at Pointe de Lévy and the guns on Ile d'Orléans were firing furiously. In the basin of Quebec every ship under Saunder's command was raging at the Beauport coast, while signals flashed and flares revealed the men clambering into landing-craft. The guns on Holmes's frigates were flashing too, and even the few men left on the other shores of the river were shooting off their muskets excitedly into the night sky. The French in reply let loose a cannonade from every gun. The batteries in Quebec, at Beauport and Samos, were all in ferocious life.

138

The sky was like blood with the reflection of the constant gun flashes; and the air was thick with smoke and the smell of powder. The noise was tremendous.

At the bottom of the Anse au Foulon the empty landing-craft were already returning to the packed transports for Townshend's reinforcements and for the men under Colonel Burton's command on the south bank of the river.

The confusion of the ascent was appalling. Men stumbled and fell, twisted their ankles, dropped their weapons. And on reaching the top the triumphant assault party was mistaken for the enemy and fired on. But the constant shouts of sergeants and officers soon collected the men together in their proper places once the summit had been reached.

The first unit to form up on the cliff-top was Colonel Howe's light infantry, and this Wolfe immediately sent to attack and silence the French batteries at Samos, where a thirteen-inch mortar and four twenty-four-pounders were firing at the packed boats of the invading army. Meanwhile hundreds more troops were swarming up the cliff in the growing light, encouraged by sailors at the water's edge swearing and shouting at them, cheering derisively when a soldier missed his foothold and stumbled to his knees.

By dawn when the last sweating soldier hauled himself on to the summit of the cliff the battery at Samos had been silenced, and unless Bougainville came up from Cap Rouge and attacked his rear Wolfe could form his army up undisturbed; for as yet the plains before him were open and undefended and the French were nowhere to be seen. There were now about four thousand, eight hundred British troops on the northern shore. Quickly and expertly, as if on parade, the regiments of the line marched off in the gathering light towards the St Foye Road to form up in the positions which they had been ordered to occupy.

When they reached the St Foye Road they wheeled to the right and advanced to a group of buildings known on

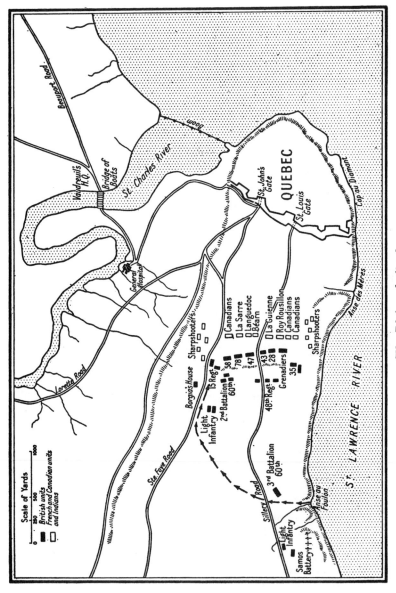

The Plains of Abraham

Dispositions of the armies, 13 September, 1759.

Wolfe's map as Borgia's House. Here they deployed to the right until they formed a line parallel to the walls of Quebec and about three-quarters of a mile from them. Then they marched in line a hundred yards nearer Quebec and halted, with their left two miles from the River St Charles and their right on the edge of the cliff. The front line was over half a mile wide and owing to the necessity of protecting the flanks and rear it was stretched very thin. Nowhere was it more than two ranks deep.

On the right of the front line were the grenadiers with the 28th Regiment on their left, and on the left flank was the 47th Regiment with the 43rd on their right. The 15th and 35th Regiments and a battalion of the 60th formed up behind them as the second line, and a little later the 58th and 78th marched through the second line to strengthen the front. A battalion of Royal Americans was left at the top of the Anse au Foulon to guard the landing-place; Colonel Burton with the 48th Regiment stayed in reserve; while a hundred and seventy men of the light infantry occupied a chain of houses near Samos to withstand a possible counter-attack on the battery which they had captured and to protect the rear of the left flank. The remainder of the light infantry under Colonel Howe formed up along the St Foye Road to withstand any French attack from the north. To prevent the enemy attempting to out-flank his right, Wolfe sent forward a company of the 28th and two platoons of grenadiers beyond the front line and along the edge of the cliff. Wolfe, Monckton, and Murray were in the front line; Townshend was in command of the second.

Soon after dawn a light rain began to fall. About six o'clock the soldiers in the front rank of the first line, standing shoulder to shoulder, caught their first sight of the white uniforms of the enemy milling round a ridge some six hundred yards in front.

Montcalm, who had heard the furious cannonade from

the battery at Samos suddenly stop, was still waiting for the return of an aide whom he had sent to Vaudreuil for information. But Vaudreuil had no idea what was happening until, at about half-past six, a breathless French officer who had seen, through the windows of the General Hospital, the British forming up on the plains to the south, burst in upon him with the information that the English had landed. Almost at the same time a message came from Quebec that a fugitive from Vergor's post also reported a British landing.

The horrifying news so unnerved Vaudreuil that it was minutes before he could decide what to do. Not until a quarter of an hour later did he think of sending a message to Bougainville at Cap Rouge. Eventually he sat down and in his laborious hand wrote : 'I have received, Sir, the letter which you have done me the honour to write me, together with the enclosed deposition of the deserter or prisoner. I have handed it over to M. le Marquis de Montcalm. It seems quite certain', he added, almost as if it were an afterthought, 'that the enemy has landed at the Anse au Foulon.'

Montcalm by this time had decided to ride over to Quebec to see for himself what the position was. He was accompanied by the Chevalier Johnstone, a Scottish officer who had gone to France after the defeat of the Jacobites at Culloden and had been given a commission in the French Army. Both men were tired, for they had spent most of the night inspecting the outposts on the Beauport cliffs where Saunders's bombardment and play with the landing-craft and marking-buoys had led them to believe that the attack was intended. After calling for a quick cup of tea at Montcalm's lodgings they rode across the Beauport River towards Vaudreuil's house.

As they approached it a messenger galloped up with the news of the English landing. At first Montcalm supposed that the assault above the town was a feint and that the main attack would still be attempted along the Beauport coast. But when he reached the path up to Vaudreuil's house he changed his mind. From here the ground fell away to the bridge of boats across the St Charles River, and he had a clear and unobstructed view over the river as far as the Plains of Abraham behind Quebec. He could see quite clearly the long, thin red lines of soldiers stretching across the plain from the St Foye Road to the cliffs overhanging the St Lawrence River. The English soldiers stood there motionless under the threatening sky and in the gentle rain as if waiting patiently for a review. The Regimental Colours drooped against their corded staves. Occasionally an officer ran across the front and there was some desultory firing from the right, where a group of Canadians was bravely and unsuccessfully trying to turn the outstretched flank. And on the left the pipers of the Highlanders were already producing their first dirge-like skirls. But the inescapable impression which the army gave was of calm patience, stillness, and unnerving quiet.

'*C'est sérieux*,' Montcalm said, as if Johnstone could doubt the fact, and immediately sent him off to call up the troops from Beauport to the St Charles River and to ask Governor Ramezay for twenty-five field-pieces from the Quebec garrison. The units on the right he could see were already moving forward. There was nothing more at the moment to be done. The English had scored a triumphant advantage by landing so many men unopposed in the night, and it would now need all his skill to dislodge them. As he sat in his saddle staring contemplatively at the British lines below him, Vaudreuil came out of his house, and the two men spoke together for a few moments. Then Montcalm rode off, crossed the St Charles, and galloped into Quebec and out again towards the Guienne Regiment forming up along the ridge south of the Sillery Road. From here he could see more closely the still motionless and silent ranks of the English stretching across the plain to the south-west. They might have been made of lead. He could hear the plaintive cacophony of the bagpipes, the occasional shot of a sharpshooter, and sometimes the excited cry of a Mohawk guide. And then the guns in Quebec began firing at the British line, and the noise of exploding shells once more washed other sounds from the air.

At Beauport Johnstone was delivering his message to Colonel Poulariez. Poulariez asked him to repeat it in front of Sennerzergue, Montcalm's second-in-command, and Lotbinière, Vaudreuil's Canadian aide-de-camp. Johnstone exasperatedly repeated that Montcalm's orders were that the troops at Beauport should immediately come back to Quebec to join the rest of the army. Poulariez then explained that he had just received orders from Vaudreuil that no troops were to leave the Beauport shore. Sennerzergue suggested that Johnstone should take them to Montcalm despite Vaudreuil's order, but Johnstone said that it was plainly not his duty to take such a responsibility but he thought that Sennerzergue should. When Johnstone rode away they were still arguing.

Montcalm had also met with infuriating procrastination. Ramezay, who had just rushed back from the General Hospital where he had been convalescing after a serious illness, had learned from Bernetz, the acting Governor of Quebec, that Montcalm had asked for twenty-five guns from the garrison. Ramezay decided that they could not be spared and sent only three.

In this atmosphere of confusion and lack of trust Montcalm called a meeting of his staff officers to decide on a plan of action. Should he attack now, he proposed to them, or wait till Bougainville received news of the English landing? The messenger would not reach the headquarters at Cap Rouge for another hour, and it might be two more before Bougainville was ready to attack. During that time the English would perhaps be reinforced. They might also drag field-pieces up the cliffs and even start digging in and building fortifications. On the other hand if he attacked now, before the English had had an opportunity to improve their position, he would attack without either Bougainville or the units which Vaudreuil was so far withholding from him, and consequently so far as it was possible for him to say, his forces would be outnumbered by the enemy.

His officers, afraid that if the army were not committed to action now, Vaudreuil might come up and issue some futile orders, suggested an immediate attack and promised Montcalm their loyal support whatever happened. Montcalm accepted their advice and prepared for battle.

To his devoted officers the Marquis had never seemed more noble. He knew the risk he was taking and that if he attacked immediately he would be fighting at a grave disadvantage. He had only five regiments of French regulars with which to fight the most important battle of his life. The rest of his men were ill-trained Canadians and Indians, brave and tough, but unused to fighting the sort of battle which the English were forcing upon him. If the defence of Quebec had been left to his unquestioned care his staff felt sure that the English army would not be in the position from which it now threatened him. If only the Canadians could have maintained a careful watchfulness for two or three more weeks the English would have had to go! His position was not only dangerous but mortifying, but he accepted it as he found it and did not waste a moment on excuses, recriminations, or regrets.

'He rode a black or dark bay horse along the front of our line', a Canadian militiaman afterwards remembered, 'waving his sword as if to excite us to do our duty. He wore a coat with wide sleeves which fell back as he raised his arm and showed the white linen of his wrist band.'

By nine o'clock the French forces were drawn up about five hundred yards in front of the walls of Quebec. Owing to the dense shrubbery the battalions could not form up in the neat, extended line that the enemy had adopted, and some companies were still in marching order, separated from each other by dense clumps of alder, hawthorn, and choke-cherry. Most of the others were in line, six men deep.

In the centre, on either side of the Sillery Road, were the regiments of La Guienne and Béarn. To their right were the regiments of Languedoc and La Sarre and to their left the Royal Rousillon Regiment, a splash of blue in the line of white and grey. On either flank were units of Canadian militia and bands of Indians. Indian and Canadian sharp-shooters were also in the scrubland and cornfields beside the St Foye Road and amongst the bushes in front of the French line along the summit of the cliffs. The total strength was rather more than four thousand men, so that the British slightly outnumbered them.

Although hidden from them by folds in the ground and the long uneven ridge known as the Buttes-à-Neveu, the French and Canadian soldiers could hear the bagpipes of the Highlanders scarcely more than half a mile away.

Behind them the guns fired, mournfully and regularly like the tolling of funeral bells, and the case-shot flew over their heads in the humid air. The crackle of fire from the sharpshooters crawling forward across the rough ground in front was the only other indication that the battle had begun.

The atmosphere was close and depressing. The French-men stood as the British stood, shoulder to shoulder in the rain, murmuring to each other, thinking of the leave they had been promised and now might never have, waiting with fear or pleasure, excitement or dread, for the order to ad-vance and to kill.

13

AT about half-past nine a volunteer in the 28th Regiment saw Wolfe go up to a platoon of grenadiers on his right and say something to them. He could not hear what the General said but all the men smiled ruefully and one or two of them laughed.

Wolfe's tall, thin figure was, as always, impeccably dressed. He was wearing a new uniform put on for the first time that morning. His face under the silk-edged tricorne hat was as white as his breeches, but he seemed happy and confident and anxious to fight. He walked up and down the ranks, quite regardless of danger, ignoring the sharpshooters and the exploding shells, talking to the men, nodding to the officers, as easy and gracious as a king at a garden-party. All that was best in the man was there to be seen and admired, now that he stood once more on a field of battle, so excited and unafraid ; made noble by his vision of triumph and a dream of a soldier's death.

A captain standing near him suddenly fell to the ground, shot through the lungs. When he recovered consciousness he found his General kneeling over him, gently holding his head in his arms. Wolfe thanked him for his services and told him that when he was well again he would be promoted, and he sent an aide-de-camp to Monckton then and there to make sure his promise was carried out should he be killed before the papers were signed.

Soon afterwards Wolfe himself was wounded. He was on the left flank with the 58th Regiment when a Canadian in a clump of bushes to the south of the St Foye Road fired at the tall figure in the smart new uniform. The bullet hit him in the wrist, tearing the tendons. But it was not a bad wound, and Wolfe got one of his aides to tie it up in a handkerchief and carried on as if nothing had happened.

Just after nine o'clock both armies advanced a little closer towards each other with skirmishing parties out in front. As they reached clearer ground the French were able to extend across the plain in line of battle, so that the armies now faced each other on a long front, less than six hundred yards apart.

The only real activity was on the British left, where Townshend was facing the constant fire of Canadians and Indians concealed in the woods north of the St Foye Road. Afraid that these irregulars might turn his flank, he had formed up Amherst's Regiment *en potence*, so that half the men faced north at right-angles to the main line, and sent out fighting patrols into the woods to shoot down any of the enemy that might attempt to get behind him.

One of these patrols, led by a captain of the 58th Regiment, had occupied a house at the edge of the wood. The captain, seeing a group of Canadians and Indians rushing forward to attack his regiment from the side, had led his men out of the house to head them off. The enemy then changed direction and ran away to the house which the patrol from the 58th had just left. The captain chased after them and despite the hail of fire which tore into his men as they approached the house he took them back into it, bayonets in hand, and a minute later Townshend saw the bodies of the enemy hurtling out through the windows.

Determined to deny the British the advantages of occupying any other buildings in the sector, the Canadians set fire to several houses and a mill, and billows of black smoke now poured up into the sky, giving Townshend a good screen behind which he could manœuvre unseen.

This smoke-screen gave the British another advantage also, for when, at about ten o'clock, Montcalm came up on to the crest of a ridge in the centre of the French position he could not see how far left the enemy line extended. Nor could he see anything like the full strength of the opposing army in other places. Most of the British soldiers were now lying down and were concealed in folds of the uneven ground or behind the bushes and scrub with which the plain was covered. He thought his officers had perhaps been right when they had suggested that only a part of the enemy's army had landed and that Wolfe was waiting there for reinforcements to come up. He felt quite certain then that he had no alternative but to attack as soon as the opportunity offered and his men were ready.

He scrambled down from the ridge, mounted his horse again, and rode once more across the front of his army. His men were tired, he knew, after a night spent standing-to in the entrenchments, and he wanted to be sure that they were ready for the fighting that was soon to come.

'Are you tired?' he called out as he rode by. 'Are you ready?' '*Etes-vous préparés, mes enfants?*' He was answered by cheers and shouts of support, and he rode back towards the high ground to watch for a favourable moment to order the advance. A French soldier remembered with pride how fine he looked in the green-and-gold uniform with the cross of St Louis glinting above his cuirass.

The rain had stopped, the clouds had gone, and the sun shone warmly down. The British soldiers, lying full-length in the deep prairie grass and bracken, to escape the exploding shells as much as to deceive the enemy, felt grateful for the warmth and the rest after the long, cold night in the boats and the hard climb. Occasionally a shell from Ramezay's guns burst amongst them, but the line was very long and the chances of getting hit seemed small. Only on the left, where some French field-guns, dragged over the St Charles River, were now firing on Townshend's brigade, were the casualties more than slight.

A brass six-pounder pulled up the heights after dawn by the artillery was returning the fire under the skilful and animated direction of Captain York; and a second one which had been damaged as it was tugged up from the river was repaired by the gunners soon after ten and then it too fired against the regiments of Béarn and La Guienne in the French centre. Unlike the other regiments which stretched out in line from the St Foye Road to the river at Anse des Mères, these two stood in column on either side of the Sillery Road, where the ground did not permit them to deploy. And the sick and wounded French soldiers looking across the plain from the windows of the General Hospital could see the plumes of smoke puffing up from the ground and the bodies jump and fall as the shells exploded in the clear morning light.

The long nights of duty in the entrenchments and the months without leave had made it as difficult for the French as for the British soldiers to look their best. Their pale grey coats and breeches were crumpled and soiled, their queues more black than white; but their tricornes trimmed with yellow, and their black stocks fastened behind their necks with buckles and decorated with red and yellow buttons gave at least an illusion of smartness. And on the right wing, next to the colony troops, the regiment of La Sarre looked as neat as it always did. Here the straight lines of soldiers, with their wide blue collars and their red waist-coats with white facings and yellow buttons, stood proud and still as if on parade at Versailles.

Each side watched the other waiting for the attack.

Montcalm rode up and down the French line, showing himself to his soldiers and stopping constantly to watch the English, trying to see how many there were. 'He looked sad', a French officer remembered, 'and very tired.'

Wolfe too looked tired but far from sad. A soldier who

afterwards proudly wrote that he 'was standing at this precise moment of time within four feet of the General' described how happy he looked. 'I shall never forget his look', he said. 'He was surveying the enemy with a countenance radiant and joyful beyond description.'

Nothing mattered to Wolfe now but victory. In his undisguised excitement and near-hysterical fervour he seemed unable to feel fear or to recognize danger. He walked quickly back along the line from the left where the bullet had cut into his wrist, towards the river. As he passed in front of the 43rd Regiment a shell exploded in front of him and a small piece of metal tore into his belly just below his navel. He stumbled and almost fell, but he walked on and when he took his position on the right wing between the 28th Regiment and the grenadiers no one appeared to notice that he was hurt.

Bleeding from his wrist and with a severe internal haemorrhage, he kept on his feet waiting restlessly for the French attack. He did not now have long to wait.

At about ten o'clock a party of light infantry made a feint of attacking the French centre along the Sillery Road, and as soon as they had drawn the enemy's fire retired in apparent disorder with shouts of affected panic. So realistic was their display that Wolfe was obliged to turn round and assure the men behind him that it was only a ruse to draw the French on to attack.

And the trick came off. A minute later the grenadiers saw the whole French army come towards them.

At first the advance was slow. The line of grey, white, and blue figures approached in three main groups with fixed bayonets. In most places they were six deep, but in the centre where the ground was more constricted the line was deeper. The soldiers walked with almost phlegmatic deliberation across the five hundred yards of open ground which separated the two armies. The line was more than half a mile long, and the soldiers in the front rank of each regiment were not much more than four feet apart. It seemed a solid, unbreakable phalanx. Although the going was rough and the ground uneven and broken up by clumps of bushes and scrub, the army approached in ominous silence and order. In spite of the constant cannonade from the batteries on Pointe de Lévy and from the guns in Quebec, it was possible to hear from the British lines the sharp, regular, disconcerting, hollow-sounding drum-beats and to feel the rhythm of the tramping boots on the damp earth. The British soldiers, standing up now, watched quietly, their muskets loaded with an extra ball, murmuring softly. The sun shone cheerfully down.

The Canadian troops on the wings were the first to break the regular pattern of the advancing line. As soon as the British ranks were in range they let off a scattering fire and then, following their usual custom, threw themselves to the ground behind cover before reloading. If no cover was available immediately around them they ran across the front of the French regiments, and the soldiers shouted at them to get out of the way.

As the advance continued it was possible for the French to see the full length of the enemy line and the battalions on the flanks threatening to get behind the sides of their own more constricted columns. To avert this the regiments in the centre inclined outwards in a late effort to extend the front of the advancing army, and as they did so large gaps began to appear on either side of the Sillery Road.

The armies were now less than a hundred and fifty yards apart, and the French pace quickened. The order to open fire was given and a hail of musket shots tore into the steady British line. A few men fell and the ranks closed. The officers shouted to warn the men to hold their fire.

At sight of the falling British soldiers the French let out, in curious unison, a shout of triumph and hurried forward. As they came on they loaded again, and again they fired, and once more the thin red line in front of them shook like a ripple and several more gaps formed and were immediately filled again.

'Hold your fire! Hold your fire!' The shouts of the British officers and sergeants restrained the men, who waited in angry impatience for the chance to shoot. Every man had his finger on his trigger; the French were so near now that 'you could count the buttons on their coats'; but along the whole line not a shot was fired. The magnificently disciplined troops in the straight and motionless ranks stood their ground, praying for the order to fire, cursing under their breath, watching the shouting enemy getting closer and closer and firing as they liked. The whole of the excited front rank of the French army was shooting now, and the crackle of fire was incessant. The Canadians, who did not care for these parade-ground tactics, decided that they had got quite close enough to the enemy and allowed the regulars to pass through them. The French ranks became more untidy and more confused as they pushed by the colony troops and militia, but they came on with loud shouts, firing constantly still, despite the unevenness of their line. The seventy yards of ground between the armies narrowed to sixty and then to fifty. A volunteer in the 47th Regiment remembered afterwards how sick he felt. His friend who had been standing next to him had been shot in the stomach and lay groaning on the ground, and he could not help him. Would the officer never give the order to fire? The French were less than fifty yards away now and he was sure he could not miss.

'Fire!'

It was Wolfe who gave the order and all down the line it was repeated and immediately obeyed.

The shattering volley of the hundreds of steady, waiting muskets as each regiment fired was so instantaneous that a French officer subsequently described it as being like the shots from six cannon. For their weeks of boring, constant practice the soldiers were at last rewarded.

Through the thick smoke which now hid the enemy from them they could hear the screams of pain, the shouts of alarm, and the urgent commands of the French officers. Into the smoke they fired again, and so well trained were they that this time also the crack of their guns was like a short, tremendous, barking roll of thunder. Quickly and calmly they reloaded, advanced twenty paces in accordance with the instructions of the drill book, and fired again. For several minutes the crackle and clatter of musket fire continued, and the bullets flew into the smoke and thudded into the French bodies behind it. After six minutes —some of those who were there thought it was nearer ten—the rate of fire lessened, and the clouds of white smoke slowly lifted. And through the drifting whorls the British soldiers could see for the first time the havoc that their murderous fire had caused. All down the French line as far as the eye could stretch, the bodies of soldiers, some struggling in screaming agony, some kneeling or sitting and groaning softly, many quite still, were revealed behind the gauze-like screen of smoke-filled air. Beyond them the remains of their companies stood in shocked helplessness. Already some men had turned their backs and were running helter-skelter for the walls of the town. For a few seconds the British ranks stood still, firing spasmodically but with an obvious lack of spirit. And then from the right wing Wolfe gave the order to charge, and the stolid, patient line came into sudden life. Like dogs unleashed, the soldiers rushed forward, shouting excitedly, at last within reach of those 'dastardly God-damned Frogs'.

Seeing them racing across the ground, with their bayonets flashing in the sunlight, the French soldiers ran for their lives. The only regiment which made an effort to hold its ground was the Royal Rousillon, which still stood, battered but as yet unbroken, on a shallow ridge to the south of the Sillery Road. But they were able to hold their ground here for less than two minutes, and when they too joined in the retreat all but three of their officers were either dead or wounded.

Despite the ragged line of squirming bodies which they had to stumble through, several of the hunters caught up with the hunted and cut them to the ground. The Highlanders were soon out in front, their kilts swishing around their knees, swinging their swords in the air and screaming like savages. Most of them had dropped their muskets so that they could swing their broadswords with more effect, and they rushed after the enemy, the glinting blades held high in the air, waiting the opportunity to bring them down on the back of a Frenchman. One long-legged Highlander caught up with a party of stragglers and swinging his sword in a wide circle cut two heads clean off before he fell, shot through the neck by a sharpshooter hiding in the bushes in front of him.

For although the army was in wild and disorderly flight, these brave Canadian snipers covered the retreat as best they could. Everywhere that there was cover a Canadian was likely to be hiding. And on the right flank, where Wolfe was leading the grenadiers and the 28th Regiment, there was cover in plenty. Also here was an English sergeant who had been reduced to the ranks by Wolfe and had deserted to the enemy before the demotion could take effect. He had sworn revenge, and his request to serve with a party of Canadian sharpshooters so that he might have an opportunity of shooting the General in the battle had been granted.

In that bright, gay uniform it could not be long before Wolfe was picked out and hit. Indeed, not long after he had given the order to charge and had started to lead the men on, waving his cane despite his blood-soaked wrist and the agonizing pain in his stomach, he had been shot again.

And the English sergeant afterwards claimed that it was he who had shot him. This time Wolfe was hit in the chest, and the bullet cut through his lung. He sank to his knees, and the lieutenant in the grenadiers who rushed to his help thought that he was already dead. The blood was coming out of his mouth. But he found the strength to ask the lieutenant to help him get back on his feet so that the soldiers should not see him fall.

So many men afterwards claimed that they had helped to carry the hero back to die in their arms that the next few minutes are clouded in confusion. It seems most likely, however, that he was carried out of danger by Lieutenant Brown of the grenadiers, an officer of artillery, and two soldiers, one of whom was James Henderson, a young volunteer. Brown sent for a surgeon, but Wolfe protested, 'There's no need now. It's all over with me.' And when a surgeon's mate came up he said, 'Lay me down. I am suffocating.'

They laid him down on the ground. He was scarcely conscious and his eyes were glazed in delirium. Henderson supported his shoulders and undid the buttons of his coat.

Then I opened his Breast, [Henderson later wrote home] And found his Shirt full of Blood At Which he Smiled And when he Seen the Distress I Was In, My Dear, Said he, Dont Grive for me, I Shall Be Happy In a Few Minutes. take Care of Your Self As I see your Wounded. but Tell me O tell me How Goes the Battle their, Just then Came some Officers Who told him that the Freinch had civen Ground and our Troops was pursuin Them to the Walls of the Town, he Was then Lyin in my Arms Just Expirin That Great Man Whose Sole Ambition Was his Country Glory Raised himself up on the News And Smiled in my Face.

After a few seconds, with an effort of pathetic determination, Wolfe raised himself again. 'Go to Colonel Burton, one of you lads,' he said with a concentration that was painful to watch. 'Tell him to march Webb's Regiment with all speed to Charles River to cut off retreat of the fugitives from the bridge.'

Then he turned away from them and closed his eyes for the last time. 'Now, God be praised,' they heard him murmur. 'Since I have conquered, I will die in peace.'

Meanwhile the rout of the enemy continued. In front of the St Charles River two hundred Canadians kept four times their number at bay while the French withdrew across the bridge of boats, until a concerted attack by the 58th, the 2nd Battalion of the 60th, and the Highlanders drove them back to the river line. Here they held their ground again until the Highlanders rushed at them across the open meadow and cut them apart with their swords. The Canadians were massacred, but when the brief and furious encounter was over, many of the pursuers also lay dead.

On the right Bragg's and Kennedy's Regiments were also held up by a company of Canadians in a coppice to their front and a solitary gun firing from Quebec. But within half an hour the coppice had been cleared and the pursuit continued.

It was not yet eleven o'clock. Less than an hour had passed since the French attacked, and now everywhere they were in retreat. The British in their excitement had lost all sense of order. All over the plains, they could be seen chasing French soldiers and officers, picking pockets, stuffing watches and souvenirs into their breeches, shouting at each other, running off in twos and threes in search of an enemy to kill or to plunder. Murray, who did not know whether or not to believe a rumour that Wolfe, Monckton, and Townshend were all dead, had taken charge of the pursuit and was trying to give it some cohesion and order; but without success. Wounded men limped about in all directions, the dying raised unheeded voices to the figures who ran by to fill their pockets while the going was good. Monckton was badly wounded with a ball in his chest which a surgeon had to cut out from beneath his shoulder-blade. Barré had half his upper cheek shot away and his eyeball hanging out of its socket. Colonel Carleton was also badly hurt. No one knew who was in charge of the army. Orders were half-heartedly given and immediately misinterpreted and disobeyed.

And then at a quarter to twelve Townshend received a message that Wolfe was dead and Monckton too badly wounded to succeed him. He immediately called off the pursuit and ordered all regiments to form up on the plain. The order came only just in time. A quarter of an hour later Bougainville with two thousand men, led by two hundred cavalrymen, came on to the battlefield and prepared to attack the disorderly British army from the rear.

Bougainville had not heard of the British landing until nearly nine o'clock, three hours after the light infantry under Colonel Howe had silenced his battery at Samos and occupied the houses nearby. At eleven he had reached Samos and ordered Captain Le Noir to attack the houses, but they were well defended and Le Noir lost thirty men in repeated, unsuccessful attempts to retake them. By now Bougainville had collected a considerable force from his outposts along the river, and he decided to leave the English in possession there and go to the help of Montcalm.

Townshend saw the blue-coated French cavalry riding out of the woods to the west, and he had no means to withstand them. He gave urgent orders to his aide-de-camp to tell the battalion commanders that the position was serious and that they must bring up their regiments without delay. He also told a runner to fetch up the two guns which had been firing on the French lines earlier on in the day and any other field pieces which might now be available. But when the artillerymen came up with the guns they brought the wrong ammunition, and the shells had to be lobbed over towards the French like mortar bombs and no accuracy of aim was possible. At length one battalion came up and soon after a second one, and Townshend was able to present some sort of front to Bougainville.

To Townshend's surprise, the threat was effective. Bougainville decided that, rather than risk an attack then and there, he would preserve what remained of the French army and retreated northwards towards Ancienne Lorette.

The French camp was panic-stricken. Montcalm had been forced back by the tide of retreating soldiers towards the gates of Quebec, and as he neared it he had been badly wounded in the chest by an exploding shell. Not wanting to let his terrified men see how seriously hurt he was, he asked two soldiers to hold him on to his saddle until he was out of their sight behind the walls of the town. A group of women saw him as he came through the St Louis Gate and one of them screamed, '*Oh! Mon Dieu! Mon Dieu! Le Marquis est tué.*'

'*Ce n'est rien*', he told them. '*Ce n'est rien. Ne vous affliquez pas pour moi, mes bonnes amies.*'

He was taken to the house of a surgeon and was told, when he asked, that he was going to die.

His second-in-command, Sennerzergue, was also dying, and St Ours, who should have succeeded him, was seriously wounded. With Lévis in Montreal there was no one able to stop the wild retreat and bring the army to order.

Johnstone said that when he reached the bridge of boats over the St Charles River he found a squad of soldiers there with orders to demolish it, although not half the French army had yet got safely across it. The soldiers already had axes in their hands. Johnstone and two other officers forced their way through the packed and pushing crowds of fugitives, shouting above the din to stop the soldiers cutting down the bridge before it was too late.

Vaudreuil had completely lost control of the situation and of himself. According to Johnstone, he had no ideas of his own on what to do. He 'listened to everybody and was always of the opinion of him who spoke last'. He had only decided to come on to the battlefield after the French had begun their last advance and now blamed 'M. le Marquis who unfortunately made his attack before I had joined him'.

When Johnstone went into his house Vaudreuil shouted at him to get out as he had no right there. In the room with Vaudreuil, Johnstone had seen Bigot, the Intendant, with a pen in his hand, and he suspected that they were drafting the terms upon which they would agree to a general capitulation. He left the house in disgust and outside saw Poulariez and Colonel Dalquier and begged them to go into the house and try to bring 'Vaudreuil to his senses'.

Then Johnstone, alone and in despair, wandered away to Beauport. He had a 'very heavy heart', he wrote afterwards, 'for the loss of my dear friend, Monsieur de Montcalm. I was sinking with weariness and lost in reflection upon the changes which Providence had brought about in the space of three or four hours.'

Meanwhile Vaudreuil had been persuaded to hold a council of war at his headquarters and to ask Montcalm for his advice. Montcalm sent a note in reply to say that Vaudreuil had only three alternatives. He could either pull the army together and counter-attack immediately, retreat to Jacques-Cartier to reform and fight again another day, or he could surrender.

When these suggestions were presented to the council of officers at Vaudreuil's house, each one was greeted with shouts of approval or disdain. Everyone spoke at once in the wildest excitement. When it became apparent that the general opinion was that the army should retreat, Bigot and Vaudreuil decided to suggest that they ought to stop to fight. The thought of serving under Vaudreuil so alarmed the officers that they came out more determinedly than ever for a withdrawal to Jacques-Cartier. Having made the protest which he, no doubt, hoped would be remembered to his credit, Vaudreuil gave in with a fine display of resignation.

'My love for the service and for the Colony', he reported later to his Minister in Paris, 'made me subscribe to the opinion of the council. In fact if I had attacked the English against the advice of all the principal officers, their ill will might have resulted in my losing the battle and the Colony also.' He was quite sure that if he 'had been the sole master, Quebec would still belong to the King'. But as it was Montcalm had given way to panic and there was nothing that he could possibly have done to save the disintegrating army except to order its withdrawal to a more defensible position.

At nine o'clock in the evening the order to retreat was given. The garrison and people of Quebec were abandoned.

14

ALL afternoon the British troops had been busy improving their position, building entrenchments and redoubts, bringing up cannon from across the river and starting work on the groundings for a battery which it was hoped would soon hammer the town into surrender. They had occupied the General Hospital on the southern bank of the St Charles River and taken prisoner all the sick and wounded soldiers who had watched the morning's battle from its windows. 'Every coppice, bush or other cover that stood on our ground this morning', Captain Knox reported, 'were cut down before night for new works.' Every house was fortified; sentries were posted on every ridge.

Burial parties worked ceaselessly to get the dead underground before nightfall, when the Indians would come out to scalp them. A nun in the Hospital watched these parties at work and felt sickened by the sight. 'All along the battlefields of the Plains', she wrote, 'still reeking of blood and covered with the slain, the victors were opening the turf, to hide from view the hideous effects of war.'

At dusk the burials were still not finished and scores of soldiers could be seen wandering about amongst the bodies in the gathering darkness, looking for loot and souvenirs. A volunteer who had been among a party of seamen landed that morning at the Anse au Foulon told a friend that he had walked over the battlefield and been shocked by the grisly sight of the corpses, hacked and mutilated by the Highlanders' swords. 'The bullet and bayonet are decent deaths', he thought, 'compared with the execution of these swords. Happy in escaping unhurt, I traversed the field of battle, while strewed with bleeding carcases, and covered with unemployed arms. A neat silver-mounted hangar, fastened to the side of an apparently headless trunk, which consequently was useless to its original French possessor attracted my attention. When the body was turned over in order to unbuckle the belt, my astonishment was indeed great : his head lay underneath his breast ; one stroke upon the back of his neck, having cut through the whole, except a small part of the skin of the throat, by which it remained connected with the body.'

Behind the corpses and the soldiers crawling about on their grim, illicit errands the British camp was quiet. A soldier of the 60th who had deserted to the enemy and been wounded in the battle, had just been found guilty after a hasty court-martial and had been summarily shot.

Fifteen hundred yards from the walls of Quebec the long line of entrenchments was already formidably strong. Most of the troops were asleep, some were talking softly. The men on guard, nervous as ever of the Indian scalping-knives, longed for their reliefs to come and a chance to sleep. Townshend was writing his instructions for the following day. 'The General Officers', he wrote in an Order whose generosity was afterwards forgotten in the ill-tempered bickering, 'wish that the person who lately commanded them had survived so glorious a day, and had this day been able to give the troops their just encomiums.'

In Quebec Montcalm was dying. Ramezay, who had been unable to get any sense out of Vaudreuil, had in desperation asked him for orders. But so near his death Montcalm could no longer be bothered with the problems of life. For the sake of an ungrateful Canada and his own ambition and sense of duty he was going to die without ever seeing his beloved France and his adored family again. Not long before he had written home and told his wife, 'The moment I see you once

163

more will be the happiest of my life. . . . I believe I love you more than ever.'

He replied to Ramezay with pathetic bitterness : 'I will neither give orders nor interfere any more. I have much to do of greater importance than your ruined garrison and this wretched country. My time is short. I hope you get out of your difficulties.'

With the nuns of the Ursuline Convent by his bedside he prayed aloud for absolution. Now and then he broke off to murmur a message for his wife or his children. He died at four o'clock in the morning.

When the sun came up both the garrison in Quebec and the soldiers in the British lines looking north towards the Beauport shore, thought that the French army was still there. Their camp looked undisturbed. The tents stood as before in rows and groups along the road to Montmorency, and the guns still lined the high-water mark across the St Charles River. But the tents were empty and the guns unmanned. The French army had gone, the militiamen had deserted, and Quebec was marooned and surrounded. As they had left their guns Ramezay hoped that they might have left their provisions also, and he sent out a party of men to bring in all the food they could. But the Indians and the starving country people had been there first, and the store-houses were empty. Unless the French came back to counter-attack it could only be a question of time before the garrison was forced to surrender. In fact Ramezay had been ordered by Vaudreuil to do so 'as soon as provisions fail' and not to 'wait until the enemy carries the town by assault'.

The French were now at Jacques-Cartier, thirty miles away. Lévis had come up from Montreal on receiving news of the battle and he did not hide his contempt for what Johnstone called the 'disgraceful rout'. He told Vaudreuil that the army must be re-formed and return to Quebec immediately. A hundred Canadian horsemen were sent back to the beleaguered town with bags of biscuits slung across their saddles and with orders for Ramezay to hold out, for the French were coming back.

Townshend was busy preparing to meet them. The troops were kept hard at work improving the lines and entrenchments, bringing over cannon, supplies, and ammunition. The sun, which had shone so cheerfully for the battle, had now gone in and for the next few days it was cloudy and wet and a strong wind blew. On the morning of 14 September the men were promised a gill of rum each day and 'new provisions the day after next'. It seemed a poor reward for their constant labour, and they resented being kept so constantly at work.

Discipline as usual after an easy victory was becoming lax. Whenever the soldiers could slip away unseen on a looting expedition they ran off to poke about in ruined houses and deserted farms and came back, their uniforms bulging with useless plunder. Townshend's orders became more and more severe. He was determined, he told the men, to use whatever means he could to prevent their 'great disorders' and to 'preserve the same good discipline kept up by their late General'. But despite the attitude of the men, the damp and blustery weather, and the still incessant bombardment from Quebec, Townshend had extended his position by 17 September to the banks of the St Charles River on the north and to within musket shot of the walls of Quebec on the south.

In the town Ramezay was besieged with requests to capitulate. No news had yet been received from outside. And as the officers of the garrison told him, for all they knew Quebec had been left to starve. There was practically no food left; living conditions were appalling; over half the houses were destroyed; Townshend's trenches were getting closer and closer to the walls below them.

On the evening of 17 September seven British ships were seen moving towards the Lower Town. At the same time a column of troops advanced across the meadows down by the St Charles River as if to attack the Palace Gate. Drums beat an alarm in the streets, but the garrison officers told Ramezay that they would not ask their men to die in a cause which the French army had already given up as lost. An artillery officer told them that they ought to feel ashamed of themselves for such defeatism. The argument lasted for several minutes. Tempers were lost. Johannés, the old Town Major, who was for defending Quebec to the last man, hit two of the more nervous officers over the head with the flat of his sword.

In the end the white flag of surrender was hoisted, but before anyone could prevent him Johannés had pulled it down again. It was hoisted once more, and in order to get him out of the way Ramezay offered Johannés the job of arranging the terms of capitulation. The Town Major, hoping that he could spin out the negotiations until help arrived, accepted a task which he thought unnecessary and 'a disgrace to the name of France'.

He arrived in Townshend's camp in an extreme ill-temper. He was slow and deliberate and refused to be hurried. He affected deafness and pleaded a lack of authority to settle certain vital terms of reference. Losing patience with him, Townshend told him that unless the far from severe terms of surrender were signed by eleven o'clock that night the town would be taken by storm. The terms were generous because Townshend's position was not nearly so strong as he pretended. Although only 58 men had been killed in the battle, as many as 597, owing to the numbers of partly spent bullets flying around the plains, had been wounded; and since the battle another 36 men had been killed by the guns in Quebec, now firing at such close range. The French losses of about 150 killed and 700 wounded were certainly greater, but if Lévis persuaded the army to return, the French would outnumber the British, who would have no line of retreat.

Johannés sulkily reported the terms and conditions of surrender to Ramezay, who considered them reasonable. Townshend agreed to the French troops and sailors being accorded the full honours of war and a safe return to France, while the civilians were guaranteed that neither they nor their property would be harmed nor their religion interfered with.

Ramezay signed the document immediately, and Johannés unwillingly took it back to the British lines. As he handed it to Townshend, the Canadian horsemen trotted into Quebec with their bags of biscuits and their promises of help. They were little more than half an hour too late.

On the afternoon of the following day a detachment of artillery rumbled into the town with a single gun and British colours flying on its carriage. In a brief and formal ceremony the keys of Quebec were handed to Townshend. At four o'clock the Bourbon flag was lowered from its mast on the citadel and the Union Jack was hoisted in its place. The siege was over.

15

O N 20 September Townshend wrote a letter to his wife to give her news of the victory and to tell her that he would soon be coming home.

MY DEAREST LIFE MY DEAREST CHARLOTTE [he wrote]

We have gained a Great Day, the particulars you will read in the public Gazette. Tho I was not in the warmest part of the action; yet I had more shotts near me than in any other action I've seen. It has pleased God to preserve me for my Charlotte and my George and the rest and to restore me to you whom alone I have found good and grateful to me. I have never forgot you in any part of the campaign. The command of an army is as disagreeable as any other. Men are as mean here as in any other profession.

I fear I have not time to write to any other friend. My love to them all.

GEO. TOWNSHEND.

Do not think my dear Life that any command tempts me to stay. The troops will soon go into garrison and then I can sett out with the Admiral.

I'm sure my dear little ones are well.

He did not attempt to hide his impatient anxiety to leave Canada and go home. Amherst had already given him permission to return, and it was only Monckton's request that he should not set off until the army was well established in Quebec which kept him there. He supervised with irritable impatience the levelling of the works which his men had built during the past week, the billeting of the troops in the ruined town, and the bringing up of provisions from the fleet.

It was not only the pettiness of the frustrating jobs which irritated him and made him keen to get away. Both he and Murray were conscious of the antagonism of some of the officers on the staff, who now that Wolfe was dead took it upon themselves to show their dislike and disapproval of those who had criticized his actions and character when he had been alive. As the days went by the bitterness and jealousies on both sides grew and festered. Only the good-natured Monckton was able to stay out of the dispute. He was disliked by neither faction. He had for a time annoyed Townshend by taking exception to the terms of surrender being arranged and signed without reference to him, but this was now forgotten. He had also, on the other hand, given grounds for complaint to Townshend's enemies by appearing to disagree with Wolfe occasionally, but he had disagreed nothing like as obviously or as disrespectfully as Townshend himself or Murray had. These two were the real culprits.

Being made well aware of this feeling against them, they tried to collect evidence which would prove Wolfe's indecision and lack of 'stability, stratagem or fixed intention' in case they were called upon to refute in public the charges which were being implied against them.

I shall look for the letter you mention [Murray wrote in answer to Townshend's request for one such piece of evidence]. Take a copy of it, and deposite the original with you. Since so black a lie was propagated I think myself very happy that you will be on the spot to contradict whatever Ignorance, or Faction may suggest. I have no copy of the paper I sent by you to General Wolfe concerning his scheme of landing between Pointe aux Trembles and St Augustin but the public orders are a sufficient proof of his intention to do it, and likewise of the suddenness of the thought of landing where we did. . . . I wish his friends had not been so much our enemies, his memory would probably have been dearer to his country than now it can be. We are acting upon the defensive, you have the execution of the plan, and I am well persuaded that you will manage it with as much tenderness to the memory of the poor Genll. as the nature of things will admit of. I find I am not to have the honour of a visit from you so I must take the opportunity of wishing you a good voyage and a happy meeting with your friends.

Townshend, at least, had need for defensive action. The antagonism of the officers in Canada was nothing compared with the bombshells of vituperation that were being prepared in England by the personal and political enemies both of himself and of his family. These bombshells were planned to burst over his head as soon as he stepped ashore in England and when the veneration to be accorded to his dead rival was at its most enthusiastic.

In the middle of October the hero and the villain sailed for home. Wolfe's body, clothed still in the uniform in which he had died, lay embalmed in its coffin below the lurching decks of the *Royal William*. Townshend, seasick but grateful for his release, sailed in the same ship. The news of the victory had preceded them.

On 14 October Wolfe's despatch to Pitt, written on 2 September, had been published in London. 'I wish I could upon this occasion', the General had begun it, 'have the honour of transmitting to you a more favourable account of the progress of his majesty's arms.' The despatch went on to relate the story of the disaster at Beauport at the end of July and the stalemate which had followed it. It had not only been depressing in itself, but it had seemed to prepare the country for worse news to come.

Three days later the news of the triumphant victory on the Plains of Abraham had been received and London was ecstatic with delight. 'The Park and Tower guns were fired', *The Gentleman's Magazine* reported, 'flags were everywhere displayed from the steeples, and the greatest illuminations were made throughout the city and suburbs that were ever known.' A hundred bonfires were lit in St George's Fields, fireworks and rockets leapt into the sky. People danced in Fleet Street, in Piccadilly, and down by the Bank. In taverns, gin-cellars, and coffee-houses all over London toasts were drunk on the house and patriotic songs were sung.

The rejoicings and celebrations were, however, somewhat dampened by the knowledge that a hero had died. And the next day the streets were full of ladies and gentlemen in mourning.

In Parliament Pitt made a long and emotional speech which was generally considered to be the worst of his career. It was, Thomas Gray thought, 'a studied and puerile declaration. In the course of it he wiped his eyes with one handkerchief and Beckford who seconded him, cried too and wiped with two handkerchiefs at once which was very moving.' And Walpole told his cousin, General Conway, whose conduct at Rochefort Wolfe had severely and repeatedly criticized, that the 'poor man's' life had paid 'the price of his injustice; and as his death has purchased such benefit to his country, I lament him, as I am sure you, who have twenty times more courage and good nature do too'.

And despite the welter of emotion and the memory of past rudeness or rebuff he was sincerely lamented, for he had died bravely and too young.

At seven o'clock in the morning of 17 November, when the *Royal William* sailed into Portsmouth, the harbour guns were fired at minute intervals, muffled bells rang from church steeples, flags were flown at half-mast, and an escort waited on the docks with reversed arms to accompany the cortège on its slow journey to London. The route through the harbour and town was lined with silent mourners, many of whom wept as they looked at the coffin and at the proud, sad faces of Hervey Smith and Bell, the aides-de-camp, who sat in the mourning coach which followed it.

On 20 November 'the corpse of General Wolfe was interred in a private manner in the family vault at Greenwich'.

In the atmosphere of bereavement and mourning piety Townshend's attitude throughout the campaign and his disagreements with the hero, rumours and stories of which were now spreading over London, seemed the more inexcusable. A letter which it was claimed he had written from Quebec and in which he had referred to Wolfe as 'a sure support and perpetual honour' was commonly supposed to have been forged by his brilliant brother Charles, as indeed it probably was, and gave his family's enemies a gratuitous advantage in their vendetta.

The feeling against Townshend finally culminated in the publication of an open letter to him, which was as venomous as it was wounding. The letter implied in terms of the most sarcastic irony that Townshend had shown, both by his behaviour and his despatch to the Ministry, that he was attempting to take away the credit for the victory from Wolfe and place it upon his own august shoulders. Townshend's own part in the operations had been so distinguished, it was suggested, that he had quite forgotten in his despatch to mention, except in passing, the comparatively inconsiderable services of General Wolfe. 'Some malignant spirits, indeed', the writer went on, 'were offended at your not having paid one civil compliment to the memory of General Wolfe or used one kind expression of esteem or affection with regard to his person. Surely some people are never to be satisfied. . . . Would they have a gentlemen of your birth and breeding imitate the foolish generosity of Sir William Johnson?—"I have only to regret the death of General Prideaux. I have endeavoured to pursue his vigorous measures, the good effects of which he deserved to enjoy." '

This was too much for Townshend to bear. It was both insulting and unjust. His reaction was expected and damaging. He lost his temper and sent a challenge to the Earl of Albemarle.

He felt certain that his old enemy the Duke of Cumberland was behind the insult and chose as the target for his rage the Duke's most intimate friend; although Albemarle was, in Wolfe's opinion at least, an incompetent fool and 'one of those showy men who are to be seen in palaces and courts'. It would, in fact, have been difficult to find a man less capable of writing so well composed and bitter an indictment.

Townshend felt the injustice of the insult the more sharply because he had at no time publicly spoken ill of Wolfe's generalship and had never claimed for himself and his fellow-brigadiers the credit for the suggestion of attaching above the town or for warning Wolfe against the folly of the daylight frontal attack on the Beauport shore which proved so terrible a mistake on 31 July. And only in private correspondence had he suggested that if Wolfe had adopted the brigadiers' idea of landing well above the town instead of so near it the British army not only might have straddled the French line of communications with Montreal but also would have cut off the French army from its lines of retreat to the west; and thus have forced it to fight or to starve or to surrender. In any event the stroke would have made more likely not only the fall of Quebec but the surrender of the whole of Canada. As it was, Canada was still French and Quebec was in danger of being re-taken.

In a public refutation of the insulting open letter, also probably written by his brother Charles, he agreed he had not accorded Wolfe any paeans of praise or tears of sympathy in his despatch, but protested that he did not consider these appropriate in a formal report to a Government Minister.

He could have favourably compared his own brief mention of Wolfe's death in the battle with the equally laconic comments in Monckton's covering letter and in Saunders's despatch. But he did not do so. He could, by drawing his colleagues into the dispute, have pointed out that Monckton had written, 'General Wolfe exerting himself on the right of our line, received a wound pretty

173

early, of which he died soon after'; and that Saunders with similar brevity had merely said, 'I am sorry to acquaint you that General Wolfe was killed in the action.'

Townshend had understandably limited his compliments to the brave, well-disciplined soldiers, and to the Navy without whom the whole operation would have been impossible and who were receiving an unjustly poor share of the nation's praise. Of the soldiers he had written: 'Were I really to attempt to point out the most striking cause of this successful stroke I must attribute it to the admirable and determined firmness of every British soldier in the field that day; conducted by the manifest ability of the officers at their respective posts.' Of the Navy he had said: 'I should not do justice to the admirals and the naval service if I neglected this occasion of acknowledging how much we are indebted for our success to the constant assistance and support received from them.'

His despatch was certainly not as well written as Wolfe's and made nonsense of Charles Townshend's assertion that Wolfe's despatch had been written by his brother George.

'If George wrote Wolfe's despatch, Charles', George Selwyn asked him, and it was a frequently quoted question, 'who the devil wrote George's?'

But it was not as badly written as all that and it was quite without malice. Townshend's political opponents, however, had blown it up into such a damning indictment that it was accepted as such, particularly by those who had not read it and by those who had forgotten it. And when the *Letter to an Hon. Brigadier-General* was published it was, for Townshend, the last straw.

Albemarle asked Colonel Crauford to be his second, and Townshend selected the Earl of Buckinghamshire. Townshend's choice was unfortunate, for the earl was an inveterate gossip who 'so loved a secret he could not wait to share it', and the news of the forthcoming duel was soon the talk of all the drawing-rooms in London. The captain of the guard at St James's received orders the night before the duel was due to take place to ride over to Marylebone Fields to prevent it.

At dawn he found Albemarle and Crauford waiting for the others, who arrived ten minutes after the appointed time. Townshend apologized for being late. 'Oh', Albemarle said, 'men of spirit don't want apologies; come, let us begin what we came for.'

But they never did. Captain Caswall rode up, said he was sorry to give orders to his senior officers but he was obliged to do so by command of the King, and sent the would-be contestants home.

It was an ignominious end to an unfortunate affair, and Townshend was more than ever insulted, laughed at, and scorned. He had not deserved this treatment. But there is no doubt that his own proud, scornful, and easily offended temperament was much to blame for the lengths to which it had been carried. He was more like Wolfe than he knew.

He told his brother that were it not for his family he could sometimes have wished that he had remained with Murray in Quebec.

16

I F Townshend had known the full agonies of that long
and bitter Northern winter he would have been grateful
that he did not have to endure them.

Murray's garrison of seven thousand men had lived in
a nightmare world of cold and hunger and disease. Billeted
in ice-cold, ruined buildings, they had marched out every
day into the frozen woods to cut timber, and harnessed in
pairs they had dragged it back on sledges over the snow,
holding the ropes in numb, frost-bitten fingers. In the snow-
muffled town the soldiers slipped and slithered as they ran
up and down the steep, glacial streets, their breath like steam
in the biting, cutting air, their uniforms wrapped round
with blankets and furs, the knees of the Highlanders covered
by stockings knitted by the Ursuline nuns.

As the weeks passed slowly by and the snow hardened
on the roofs and lay in deep drifts against the ramparts
and the river below them froze in a solid mass, the soldiers
sickened and died. The makeshift hospitals were crowded
to the doors. A quarter of the garrison had scurvy or dysentery and most of the others had frost-bite. By the middle of
November soldiers were dying every day in the gripping,
relentless cold. A hundred and fifty men were dead by
Christmas, nearly four hundred by the end of February,
and most of the bodies lay out in rows face down, frozen to
the snow, waiting for the spring to soften the solid ground
and their friends to shovel them into their common graves.

Slabs of gristly salt pork were the only form of food not
in short supply. But drink was plentiful, and the men
gulped down as much as they could get. When they were

drunk they looted the houses and cellars of civilians, to be punished next day by as many lashes of the cat as the surgeon considered they could stand without permanent injury.

The winter days wore on, the drunkenness increased, and the punishments grew more and more severe. Women stripped to the waist were whipped through the streets for selling rum without permission, and the sentence for robbery was death. Once two soldiers condemned to death for looting were told that one of them had been reprieved, and they squatted down on the floor of their cell to throw dice to see which of them should die.

The men longed to be sent to the General Hospital and the gentle care of the nuns, and dreaded their turns of duty outside Quebec in Murray's two fortified outposts in the churches of St Foye and Lorette, where the Indians howled all around them in the black forests like wolves.

Skirmishing parties of American rangers and light infantry went out in snow-shoes to attack French and Canadian outposts and Indian villages downriver towards Montreal, and returned with the frozen scalps of the enemy hung on their belts like sporrans. Rumours flew round the garrison that Lévis was already on the march from Montreal with hordes of Indians thirsty for revenge and blood. Messages were received from a Canadian post on Pointe de Lévy that 'a large company of expert hairdressers' were ready to wait upon the British troops in Quebec as soon as spring came or earlier if their 'services should be required'. The cold was deepened by fear.

At the end of March the biting, cruel cold grew less intense and the snow began to slip from the roofs and spatter into the slushy streets. By the middle of April the solid ice on the river had cracked and broken up, and the St Lawrence was once more navigable by small ships.

A little after midnight on 25 April as a south-easterly wind howled down the river and the waters were lashed by a fierce storm, Captain Macartney of the frigate *Racehorse* was told by the watch that a man's voice shouting for help could be heard through the rushing spray. He ordered a midshipman to take out six sailors in a boat and to bring the man aboard. The boat bumped out into midstream, between the hunks of drifting, cracking ice, as the sailors called out into the darkness. They found the man clinging half dead to an ice floe, swirling downstream on the ebb tide. He wore the uniform of a French sergeant of artillery. He was given a mug of rum and wrapped in a blanket while a sailor rubbed his frozen limbs. When he could talk he told Captain Macartney that his boat had overturned in the storm when his regiment was trying to land on Cap Rouge and that all his companions had been drowned. A French army of twelve thousand men, he said, were marching on Quebec under the Chevalier de Lévis.

Murray was woken at three o'clock in the morning and told the news. The dreaded battle could no longer be avoided. He ordered an immediate stand-to and marched out of Quebec at dawn to withdraw his outposts. The storm had passed and the morning was cold with a drizzling, persistent rain and his wet boots slithered in the slush and mud. He pulled back the outposts, blew up the buildings and churches in which the ammunition had been stored, and came back to Quebec in an anxious and dispirited mood. Of the seven thousand men left under his command in the previous October he now had scarcely three thousand fit for action, and most of these were far from well. But he knew that he must come out and fight, for the walls of the town could not withstand a siege and the ground was still too hard to make entrenchments outside them.

At half-past six in the morning of 27 April he came out with all the men he could muster, including several who had been in hospital the night before but had volunteered for duty and even a few cooks and sutlers.

The Plains of Abraham were grey with slush as the British line formed up on the Buttes-à-Neveu, where Montcalm had started his attack in the September before. The French were not yet in position, so Murray ordered a further advance and then unlimbered his cannon. At sight of the long, orderly line and the threatening guns Lévis ordered his left flank to withdraw to the woods ; and Murray, taking advantage of this and perhaps mistaking it for a retreat, ordered a third advance. It was a grave and fateful error.

Murray by advancing again had abandoned his favourable position for the difficult, sloping ground beyond the higher plateau. His troops, particularly on the right wing, became bogged down in the knee-deep slush. The guns too stuck and slithered in the mud, and the ammunition-carts sank past hope of recovery in the drifts and pits of snow.

The ensuing battle was brief and bloody. On both wings the British attacked in furious desperation and were as furiously repulsed. On the right the light infantry assaulted a windmill and occupied it for a few minutes until five companies of French grenadiers under Colonel Dalquier, with a bullet in his chest, counter-attacked and overwhelmed them, killing all but four of their officers. On the left a group of American rangers under the young Moses Hazen (later to become a general in the Revolutionary army) and a company of a hundred volunteers under Major MacDonald captured two blockhouses built by the British in the previous autumn. But they too fell back after a ferocious French counter-attack in which Hazen was badly wounded and MacDonald was killed.

Murray soon realized the hopelessness of his position. He was outnumbered two to one, and he had lost the advantage of superior artillery and better ground by his anxious and precipitate attack. After two hours of violently bitter fighting both sides had lost more than a thousand men, and Murray ordered a retreat.

The men scrambled back, carrying as many of their wounded as they could, to the temporary safety of the walls.

How long he could hold out Murray dared not estimate.

He had lost that morning most of his best men. The rest, as Sergeant Johnson of the 58th reported, were 'half-starved, scorbutic skeletons . . . too few and too weak to stand an assault'. But Murray was determined to make amends for the disaster and gave an example to his men of steadfast cheerfulness, confidence, and courage. He put everyone to work. By the gates of the town hundreds of gaunt, pale convalescents filled sandbags and cut fascines for the gun emplacements on the ramparts; in the hospitals the wounded and the sick rolled bandages and made wadding for the cannon. The fitter men cut embrasures along the walls, built overworks, and hammered *chevaux-de-frise* into the exposed gaps. The officers worked as hard as the men, to the horror of the conservative Sergeant Johnson. 'None but those who were present on the spot', he wrote, 'can imagine the grief of heart the soldiers felt to see their officers yoked in the harness, dragging up cannon from the Lower Town; to see gentlemen, who were set over them by his Majesty to command and keep them to their duty, working at the batteries with the barrow, pickaxe and spade.'

Murray maintained a discipline of the strictest severity. The six hundred women attached to the army, not one of whom died in the appalling winter conditions and only a few of whom had been slightly ill, were kept firmly in their place. The rum barrels of sutlers who got the men drunk were staved in. Looters were publicly hanged in the squares and their bodies left swinging from the rough-hewn gallows. Men convicted of insubordination were sentenced to a thousand strokes of the lash or shot out of hand.

On the plains below them Lévis was busy too. He was building deep entrenchments on the stony ground of the Buttes-à-Neveu; and his men were building scaling ladders and petards. But owing to the constant, sharp fire from the British garrison it was not until the beginning of May that the French had finished their own batteries and their guns replied. From now on the fire on both sides was ceaseless, broken occasionally when flags of truce were hoisted and Lévis sent Murray a wagonload of spruce boughs with which the English commander could brew his favourite beer ; or Murray sent Lévis a Cheshire cheese in exchange for a brace of partridges.

Both commanders watched the river anxiously, for on that everything depended. If the French fleet sailed through the now quickly thawing channel first, the British would be forced to surrender ; if the British were the first to come, the siege would have to be lifted. Every day Murray walked from his headquarters in St Louis Street and looked down from the ramparts into the Basin of Quebec and at the clear, untroubled waters, empty except for the *Racehorse* and the few other small ships which were all that had so far come through.

On 9 May an officer burst into Murray's headquarters and told him that a big man-of-war was sailing up the river. Murray rushed out and gave orders for British colours to be hoisted on Cap au Diamant. The ropes had broken but an agile sailor shinned excitedly up the pole and unfurled the Union Jack in the gentle breeze.

As the ship sailed slowly into the basin the men of the garrison ran to the walls of Quebec and climbed on to the top of the ramparts to watch it, ready to cheer or curse. Cannon were trundled from their emplacements on the western walls and their waiting barrels levelled at it, in case it should turn out to be French. An officer peering through a telescope saw the ship's colours being hoisted and wondered, with his heart in his mouth, whether they would be the red of England or the white of France, whether Wolfe and the hundreds of men killed outside the walls would have died in vain and Quebec would be lost again.

A few seconds later the red cross of the British flag unfurled above the top-sail. It was the *Lowestoft*, and she gave the British garrison a twenty-one-gun salute as the soldiers jumped up and down on the walls, waving their hats in the air, shouting and cheering at the top of their voices. The wounded men hobbled out of the hospitals to join in the cheering and waved their bandaged stumps and their hand-carved crutches as the tears trickled down their hollow cheeks.

A few days later the *Diana* and the *Vanguard* sailed into the basin, and the *Lowestoft* sailed into the upper river to drive the French ships out of it. Lévis had no alternative but to lift the siege and retreat to Montreal. Another siege was over.

And the war was nearly won. In the middle of May the French army, weak and exhausted, tumbled into Montreal, all the Canadian units having deserted on the way.

Two months later Murray with two thousand, five hundred men, refreshed by the pleasant summer weather and the fresh food from the ships, sailed quietly and confidently up the St Lawrence River after them. 'Nothing', Captain Knox thought, 'could equal the beauties' of the navigation. 'The meandering course of the channel, so narrow that an active person might have stepped ashore from our transports either to the right or left; the awfulness and solemnity of the dark forests with which these islands are covered, together with the fragrancy of the spontaneous fruits, flowers, and shrubs; the verdure of the water by the reflection of neighbouring woods, the wild chirping notes of the [birds]; the masts and sails of ships appearing as if among the trees, both ahead and astern, heightened by the promiscuous noise of the seamen and the confused chatter of the rapturous troops on their decks formed all together . . . an enchanting diversity.'

The enjoyable voyage was soon over and the convoy dropped anchor at the island of St Thérèse, just below Montreal, to wait for the remaining British troops in Canada to arrive and help to squeeze the French from their last foothold in North America.

Brigadier Haviland was coming from the south with three thousand men, Amherst with eleven thousand from the west.

Haviland arrived a few days after Murray, but Amherst had a more difficult journey. The few French outposts along the St Lawrence route from Oswego caused him little trouble, but the rapids were a frightening obstacle. His men, packed into whale-boats and canoes, shot the Galops, Point Iroquois, Point Cardinal, and Rapid Plat without mishap; but twenty soldiers were lost going over the Long Sault, and three days later nearly a hundred men were drowned as their boats overturned and plunged them into the racing waters of the Cascades and Cedars rapids. By the evening of 6 September, however, the army had landed at Lachine, and Montreal was in sight.

The town was surrounded and, unlike Quebec, it did not occupy a position of any natural strength. There were only twenty-five hundred troops inside it and provisions for less than a fortnight. Outside the gates were seventeen thousand men in control of the river. On 8 September the garrison surrendered, and Vaudreuil signed the capitulation which ended for ever the power of France in America.

Almost a year had gone by since the battle on the Plains of Abraham. People in England had been horrified to learn that it had after all been merely an indecisive victory in a still continuing war. The news that Quebec had been almost re-taken by the French came as a shock to Londoners, who had taken it that the future of Canada had been settled long ago. 'Who the deuce was thinking of Quebec,' Walpole exclaimed in surprise. 'America was like a book one has read and done with. But here we are on a sudden, reading our book backwards.'

Townshend was blamed once more; this time for having let the French army escape to fight again after Wolfe had defeated it. But Wolfe himself was never blamed. Criticism of him was still considered close to blasphemy. A sensible but very guarded suggestion that if he had attacked a month earlier and several miles farther up the river, as his brigadiers had suggested, the war might have been ended a year sooner was greeted with contemptuous disdain. He was a hero and he was dead, and of such men *nil nisi bonum*. He had perished in his duty and in the service of his country. And he had never himself considered that there could be a more honourable death.

It was for that reason fortunate that he was not to know how transitory for his country the advantages of his victory were to be. He had helped to win an empire at Quebec; but another and greater empire was shortly to be lost.

For the removal of the fear of French motives and encroachments from the minds of the American colonists, and the taxes which were levied in the colonies to help pay for the costs of war, precipitated the American Revolution and the birth of the United States.

And so Wolfe had done his unwitting part in bringing the American *canaille*, whom he so much despised, a little nearer to their freedom. A few years after the end of the war in Canada the first shots of the Revolutionary war were fired at Lexington, and the Americans were on the road to their destiny.

It was, although Wolfe would not perhaps have thought so, a happy ending.

BIBLIOGRAPHY

An accurate and Authentic Journal of the Siege of Quebec (1759)*
Annual Register

Butler, Lewis, *Annals of the K.R.R.C.* (1913)
Bradley, A. G., *The Fight with France for North America* (1908)
Brodigan, F. (editor), *Historical Records of the 28th Regiment* (1884)

Correspondance de Bougainville*
Carver, P. L. (editor), *Wolfe's letters to the Duke of Richmond* (1938)
Collection des Manuscrits contenant Lettres, Mémoires, et autres Documents Historiques relatifs à la Nouvelle France, 1492-1789 (1883-1885)
Collection des Manuscrits du Maréchal de Lévis (1889-1895)
Caldwell, Sir J., *An Essay on the Conduct and Character of His Excellency Lord Viscount Townshend* (1771)
Canadian Historical Review
Cannon, Richard, *Historical Record of the 15th Regiment* (1848)
Casgrain, H. R., *Guerre du Canada* (1891)
Cauvain, H., *Dernière Campagne du Marquis de Montcalm* (1885)
Clowes, W. L., *The Royal Navy*, Vol. III (1898)
Collections of the New York Historical Society

Daniell, D. S., *Cap of Honour*. The Story of the Gloucestershire Regiment (1951)

---

* These sources, in whole or in part, are printed in volumes IV-VI of *The Siege of Quebec* (Doughty and Parmelee), 1901.

Dialogue betwixt General Wolfe and the Marquis Montcalm in the Elysian Fields (1759)

Dialogues in the Shades between General Wolfe, General Montgomery, David Hume, George Grenville and Charles Townshend (1778)

Dictionary of National Biography

Documents Relatifs à la Nouvelle France (1883)

DOUGHTY, A. G., *The Cradle of New France* (1908)

        The Fortress of Quebec, 1608-1903 (1904)

        (with DIONNE, N. E.), *Quebec Under two Flags* (1903)

        (with PARMELEE, G. W.), *The Siege of Quebec* (1901)

Edinburgh Review

English Historical Review

ENTICK, J., *The General History of the Late War*, containing its Rise, Progress and Events (1763-1764)

Extraits des Archives des Ministères de la Marine et de la Guerre à Paris—Canada (1890)

FINDLAY, James, T., *Wolfe in Scotland* (1928)

FORTESCUE, J. W., *History of the British Army*, Vol. II (1899)

FRASER, M., *Extract from a Manuscript Journal relating to the Siege of Quebec in 1759* (1867)

French War Papers of the Maréchal de Lévis (1888)

FULLER, J. F. C., *Decisive Battles of the Western World* (1955)

Galway Papers*

General Orders in Wolfe's Army during the Expedition up the River St Lawrence in 1759 (1875)

General Wolfe's Instructions to Young Officers (1768)

Gentleman's Magazine

Genuine Letters from a Volunteer in the British Service at Quebec (1761)*

GURNEY, Russell, *History of the Northamptonshire Regiment* (1935)

Histoire de la Guerre contre les Anglais (1759)
History of the 20th Regiment, 1688-1888 (1889)

JOHNSON, John, *Memoirs of the Siege of Quebec and the Total Reduction of Canada**
*Journal Abrégé d'un Aide-de-Camp**
*Journal de Bougainville**
Journal du Marquis de Montcalm (1895)
*Journal mémoratif de ce qui s'est passé de plus remarquable pendant qu'a duré le Siége de la Ville de Quebec**
Journal of Major Moncrief (1847)*
Journal of the Expedition up the River St Lawrence (1886)*
*Journal of the Particular Transactions of the Siege**
Journal of the Quebec Expedition (1759)
Journal of the Siege of Quebec in 1759
Jugement Impartial sur les Operations Militaires de la Campagne en Canada en 1759 (1840)

KNOX, John, *Journal of the Campaigns in North America* (edited by A. G. Doughty for the Champlain Society 1914).

LE MOINE, J. M., *Manuscripts Relating to the Early History of Canada* (1866-1868)
LESCARBOT, Marc, *History of New France* (1907)
Letter to an Honourable Brigadier General Commander-in-Chief of His Majesty's Forces in Canada (1760)
LEVINGE, R. G. A., *Historical Records of the 43rd Regiment* (1868)
LOWER, Arthur R. M., *Colony to Nation* (1946)
LYDEKKER, J. W., *The Faithful Mohawks* (1938)
187

MAHON, R. H., *Life of General the Hon. James Murray* (1921)

MALARTIC, le Comte Gabriel de Maurès de (and Gefferat, P.), *Journal des Campagnes au Canada de 1735 à 1760* (1890)

Manoeuvres . . . including the late General Wolfe's (1766)

Manuscripts of the Marquess Townshend (1887)

MANTE, Thomas, *History of the Late War in North America* (1772)

MARGRY, Pierre, *Relations et Mémoires inédits pour servira à l'histoire de la France dans les pays d'outre-mer, tirés des Archives du Ministere de la Marine et des Colonies* (1867)

MARTINEAU, G. D., *A History of the Royal Sussex Regiment* (1955)

MAUDUIT, Israel, *Apology for the Life and Actions of General Wolfe* (1765)

Mémoire du Sieur de Ramezay commandant à Quebec (1861)

Mémoire sur la Campagne de 1759 par M. de Johannès, Major de Quebec (1861)*

Memoirs of Major Robert Stobo (1854)

Memoirs of the Chevalier de Johnstone (translated by Charles Winchester) (1870)

Mémoires du S—— de C—— contenant l'histoire du Canada durant la Guerre (1838)

Mémoires et de Relations sue l'Histoire Ancienne du Canada (1840)

Mémoires et Documents relatifs à l'Histoire du Canada (1859)

Mémoires sur la Canada depuis 1749 jusqu'a 1760 (1838)

MONTRESOR, John, *Journal of the Siege of Quebec* (1882)*

MURRAY, Hon. James, *Journal of the Siege of Quebec* (1871)

NEWBOLT, Sir Henry, *The Story of the Oxfordshire and Buckinghamshire Light Infantry* (1915)

Newcastle Papers*

Nineteenth Century and After

Northcliffe Collection of the Public Archives of Canada (1926)

Notes and Queries

Panet, J. C., *Journal du Siége de Quebec en 1759* (1886)
A Parallel of Military Errors, of which the French and English Armies were Guilty, during the Campaign of 1759 in Canada (1866)
Parkman, Francis, *Montcalm and Wolfe* (1884)
Publications de la Société Historique de Montreal
Publications de la Société Litteraire et Historique de Quebec

Rapports de l'Archiviste de la Province de Quebec
Recueil des pièces relatives à la publication des manuscrits du Maréchal de Lévis sur la Guerre du Canada 1755-1760 (1888)
Refutation of the letter to an Honourable Brigadier General (1760)
Relation du Siége de Quebec en 1759 (1840)
Reports of the Historical Manuscripts Commission
Reports on Canadian Archives
Rogers, Robert, *Journals* (1765)
Roy, P. G., *Les Monuments Commémoratifs de la Province de Quebec* (1923)

Sackville Papers*
Samuel, Sigmund, *The Seven Years War in Canada* (1934)
Shippen, E., *Memoir of Henry Bouquet (1719-1765)* Brigadier-General in America and Colonel of the Royal American Regiment (1900)
Siege of Quebec, The by a Nun of the General Hospital of Quebec (1855)
Smith, W. J. (editor), Grenville Papers (1852-3)
Smythies, R. H. R., *Records of the 40th Regiment* (1894)

Thornton, Leslie H., *Campaigners Grave and Gay* (1925)
Townshend, C. V. F., *The Military Life of Field Marshall George 1st Marquess Townshend 1724-1807* (1901)
Townshend, George, *Journal of the Siege of Quebec*
Townshend Papers*

Transactions of the Royal Society of Canada
Trimen, Richard, *An Historical Memoir of the 35th Regiment* (1873)

University of Toronto Quarterly, The

Waddington, R., *La Guerre de Sept Ans* (1899)
Walpole, Horace, *Memoirs of the Reign of George II* (1847)
Warburton, G. D., *The Conquest of Canada* (1849)
Waugh, W. T., *James Wolfe Man and Soldier* (1928)
Webb, E. A. H., *History of the 12th Regiment* (1914)
Webster, J. Clarence, *The First Life of James Wolfe* (1930)
　　　　　　　　　　The Journal of Jeffrey Amherst (1931)
　　　　　　　　　　Wolfe and the Artists (1930)
　　　　　　　　　　Wolfiana (1927)
Whitton, Frederick E., *Wolfe and North America* (1929)
Whitworth, Rex, *Field-Marshal Lord Ligonier* (1958)
Willson, Beckles, *The Life and Letters of James Wolfe* (1909)
Winsor, John, *The Struggle in America between England and France* (1895)
Wood, William, *Logs of the Conquest of Canada* (1909)
　　　　　　　　The Fight for Canada (edition of 1905)
　　　　　　　　The Winning of Canada (1920)
Wright, J., *History of the Late War* (1765)
Wright, R., *Life of Major General James Wolfe* (1864)
Wylly, H. C., *The Loyal North Lancashire Regiment* (1933)

INDEX

192

OTHER COOPER SQUARE PRESS TITLES OF INTEREST

THE WAR OF 1812
Henry Adams
New introduction by Col. John R. Elting
392 pp., 27 maps
0-8154-1013-1
$16.95

HANNIBAL
G. P. Baker
366 pp., 3 illus., 5 maps
0-8154-1005-0
$16.95

MARGARET SANGER
An Autobiography
New introduction by Kathryn Cullen-DuPont
516 pp., 1 b/w photo
0-8154-1015-8
$17.95

CANARIS
Hitler's Master Spy
Heinz Höhne
736 pp., 29 b/w photos, 1 map, 2 diagrams
0-8154-1007-7
$19.95

Available at bookstores; or call 1-800-462-6420

Cooper Square Press

150 Fifth Avenue
Suite 911
New York, NY 10011